PEASANT
CHIC

PEASANT CHIC

A Guide to Making Unique Clothing Using Traditional Folk Designs

Esther R. Holderness

Photographs by
Joan Hadden and David Monley

Drawings by
Kaye Sherry Hirsh

HAWTHORN BOOKS, INC.
Publishers / NEW YORK

Library of Congress Catalog Number: 76-7833

ISBN: 0-8015-5811-5

1 2 3 4 5 6 7 8 9 10

To my mother,
Rachel Arloa Randolph,
who taught me to sew

CONTENTS

Skirts, Dresses, Robes

Measurement Chart and Metric Equivalents Table

Index

INTRODUCTION

The collection of designs in this book represents a fresh way of adapting timeless peasant motifs to suit current fashions and modern materials. The designs also offer an exciting alternative to mass produced, ready-made clothes—an opportunity to create one-of-a-kind garments and accessories that express one's individual style. They all are based on authentic ethnic sources, some using the actual garments as models, and others gleaned from drawings of the period. Some follow the original design exactly, others are freely adapted—and all are unique in their handcrafted, personally selected details.

This is not a how-to sewing book. It assumes that the reader has a certain basic knowledge of simple sewing terms and techniques, and an adventurous spirit. The emphasis in all these designs, whether casual or elegant, is on comfort, flair, and simplicity of construction. Most of the pattern pieces are squares or rectangles, so pattern placement and cutting are simple. Much of the actual sewing is limited to straight seams, uncomplicated facings, and hems. Because of the nature of the garments there are virtually no fitting problems to solve.

These designs lend themselves to the most imaginative choices of fabrics and trimming. Standard dress fabrics are always appropriate, but upholstery and drapery materials should not be overlooked since they offer an intriguing range of weights and textures, as do blankets and bedspreads. As far as decorative details are concerned, the variety is infinite—antique lace, buttons, beadwork; hand or machine embroidery; macrame; braid; crocheted borders; fringe; applique; ceramic, leather, or hand-carved wooden buttons; oriental frogs; ribbon and cord of every description; and so much more. Finding and combining the right fabric, trimming, and design are challenging, but the rewards of making beautiful additions to one's wardrobe are well worth the effort.

Outerwear

NORWEGIAN FISHERMAN'S JACKET

I am presenting this jacket first because its method of construction is typical of many of the following designs. Made of straight pieces and sewn together with simple seaming, decorated with cross-stitch and other easy embroidery stitches, it is a beautiful garment that will be much admired.

This is an authentic design given to me by an artist who lived in Norway for a time. She brought a jacket back with her and from this pattern I have made dozens of these jackets of many fabrics in many colors. The garment, originally designed to be stored in a seaman's chest when not in use, folds up completely flat. The jacket is comfortable, sets well on the shoulders, and the hand embroidery gives it that European peasant look that is chic and timeless.

MATERIAL REQUIRED

> 2 yards of 54″ wide wool, or 1½ yards of 60″ wide wool, or one imported wool stole
> 2 colors of yarn to blend with or dramatize fabric colors
> 1 yarn needle with a large eye
> Standard sewing thread to match fabric

Select fabric that looks handwoven, preferably with a border design. Using wide material you have enough to cut double and line the jacket with the same fabric to make a heavier, warmer garment. If you do your own weaving this is the best of all. You can make your own border design and use heavy thread so a single thickness is warm enough. If you can afford handwoven cloth, use it, as the jacket will wear for years. When using handwoven, single thickness, you will need two pieces 13½″ x 72″, cutting off the 13½″ x 18″ piece at one end of each for sleeves.

CUTTING DIAGRAM

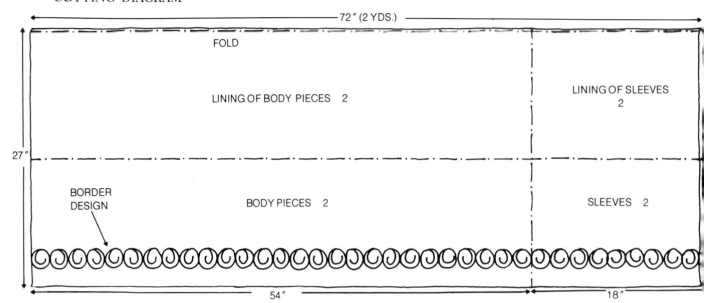

Large: cut body pieces 60″ x 14″, sleeves 20″ x 14″
Small: cut body pieces 54″ x 12″, sleeves 18″ x 12″

METHOD OF CONSTRUCTION

Place one body piece on top of the other, right sides in, aligning the edges and border print as shown in figure 1. Make a ½″ seam 22″ long along the border edge to form the back of the garment, leaving the balance unsewn for the neck and front opening (figure 2). This leaves a triangular fit at the neckline in back.

Fold the joined body pieces in half, aligning the back bottom edge with the front bottom edges (figure 3). The fold at the top is the shoulder line. Mark this point X with a pin at each outer edge.

Then find the center of each sleeve on the 18″ side opposite the border design and mark this point X with a pin (figure 4).

Place sleeve point X right side down against the right side of the shoulder line point X, pin to hold firmly in position, and machine sew the sleeve to the body of the jacket (figure 5). Attach the other sleeve in exactly the same way.

Refold the right sides together to sew the underarm and side seams (figure 6). Starting at the edge of the sleeve, sew a seam to within 1½″ of the underarm. Starting at the bottom of the side seam, sew to within 1½″ of the underarm. This leaves a diamond shape opening at the point where the sleeve joins

Figure 1

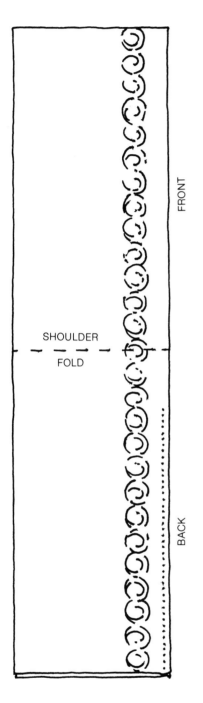

SHOULDER

FOLD

FRONT

BACK

Figure 2

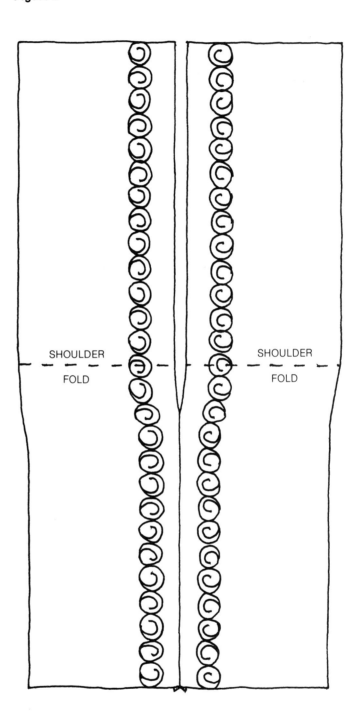

SHOULDER

FOLD

SHOULDER

FOLD

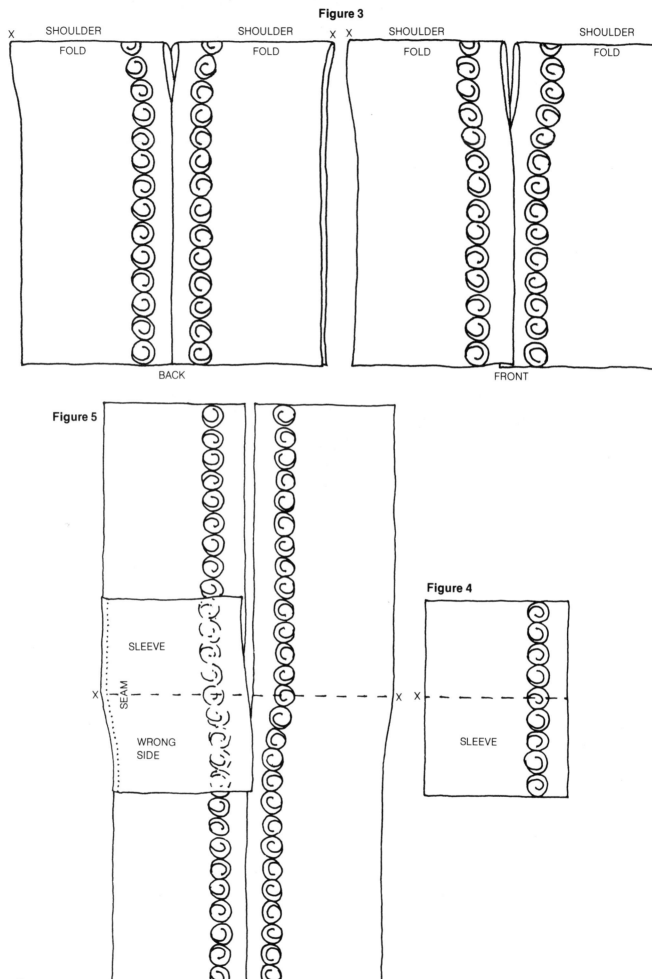

Figure 3

SHOULDER FOLD   SHOULDER FOLD   SHOULDER FOLD   SHOULDER FOLD

X   X X

BACK   FRONT

Figure 5

SLEEVE

SEAM

WRONG SIDE

X   X X

Figure 4

SLEEVE

6

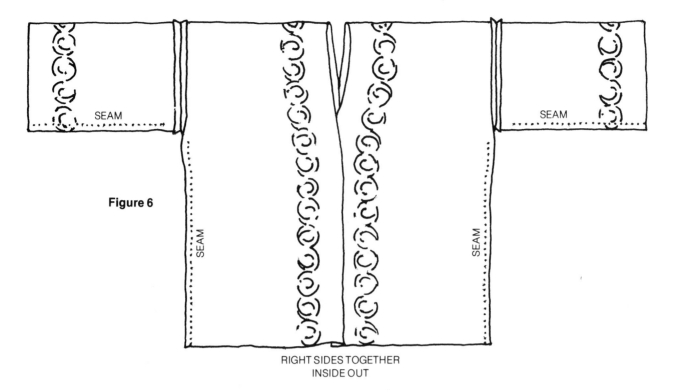

Figure 6

SEAM

SEAM

SEAM

RIGHT SIDES TOGETHER
INSIDE OUT

the body, which is correct. This is done in many peasant garments. It allows for neat, flat folding, and eases the strain where a garment usually wears out. Press the seams flat open on the wrong side when seaming is completed.

Sew the duplicate lining pieces together in the same manner. Then placing the right side of the lining to the right side of jacket, align the edges, pin into position and sew the front opening edges together.

Turn right side out and align the edges of the sleeves, keeping the underarm seams together. Turn the edges in ½". Pin together and whip stitch by hand or top stitch by sewing machine (figure 7). Turn in the edges of the underarm opening and join the jacket and lining together in the same way you handled the sleeve edges.

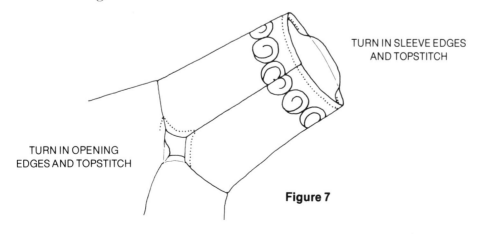

TURN IN SLEEVE EDGES
AND TOPSTITCH

TURN IN OPENING
EDGES AND TOPSTITCH

Figure 7

At this point I pull threads from both the body of the jacket and the lining at the bottom edges for 1″ of self-fringe. You can make yarn fringe but the soft effect of self-fringe is best.

Complete the jacket with embroidery. Make cross-stitches (figure 8) over all the seams and edging stitches (figure 9) along the edges of the front and sleeves. You can, of course, make the embroidery as elaborate as you wish using a variety of stitches (figure 10).

If you use an imported stole or carriage robe for the jacket it will have rolled fringe on each end which can be used for the bottom edge of the jacket if cut as shown in figure 11.

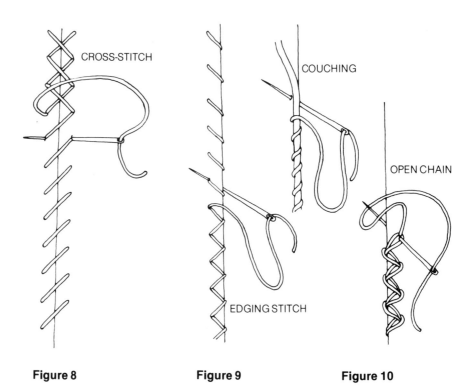

Figure 8   Figure 9   Figure 10

To make a tie belt cut 2″ off the whole length of one side of the stole before cutting the jacket. The only differences in construction will be joining the front and back pieces with a seam at the top of each shoulder and having no seam down the back. Cut a 4″ slash at the center top edge of the back to make the triangle effect of the back neckline. Machine sew zigzag stitches around the edges of the tie belt and embroider

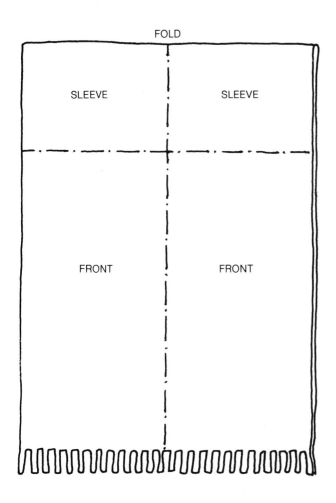

Figure 11

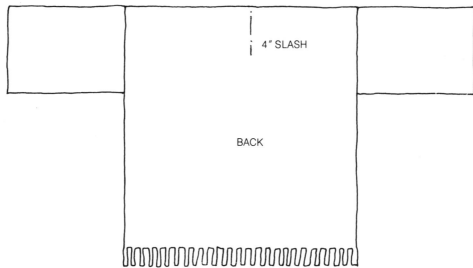

over these stitches. Add embroidery down the back just the same as if it were seamed.

Using unusual fabrics with interesting border designs adds to the pleasure of the finished garment.

ADAPTATION

You can make an adaptation of this design which gives a more conventional fit across the back by cutting the body piece as in figure 12. This makes a rounded neckline in the back with a straight opening down the front. Embroider a cross-stitch design down the middle of the back to give the same effect as the original jacket where the back seam is covered with cross-stitches.

Cut and add sleeves as in the original diagram.

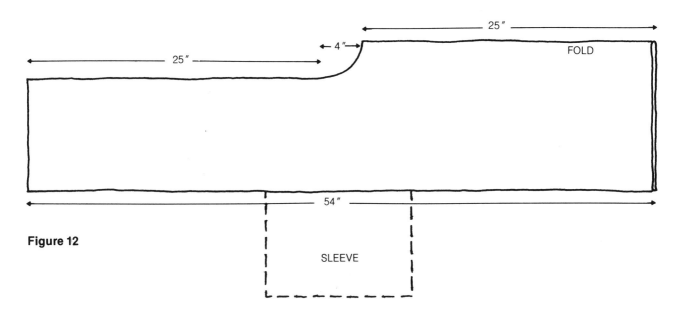

Figure 12

FOUR-SQUARE PEASANT PONCHO

Ponchos are great wraps for any time of the year. They look equally well with pants, culottes, or skirts of every length and width—and they are easy to make.

MATERIAL REQUIRED

2 yards of 36″ wide fabric or 1 yard of 60″ wide fabric

METHOD OF CONSTRUCTION

Cut eight 15″ squares. Join four of the squares as shown in figure 1, machine sewing the seams on the wrong side of the fabric. Join the other four squares in exactly the same way. These will serve as the lining.

Figure 1

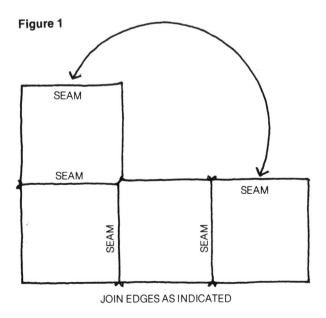

JOIN EDGES AS INDICATED

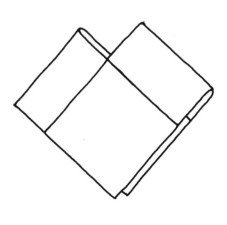

After the two sets of four are sewn, place them together, right sides in. Pin in position and machine sew all around the bottom edge, leaving the neckline edges unsewn. At this point you may want to place small darts at the middle of the shoulder squares to make the neckline fit more smoothly.

Turn right side out, turn in the raw edges at the neckline, and whip stitch into place by hand.

There are many ways to vary this versatile poncho. I made one alternating black and white squares of wool on one side, with solid black on the other side, trimmed with black wool fringe around the bottom. Plaid or patchwork squares also make attractive ponchos. Using a solid color on one side and plaid, stripes, or print on the other gives you two ponchos in one.

Another way to construct this poncho is to hem four squares by machine, using zigzag stitches, and then crochet the squares together, adding a crocheted border around the bottom. This makes a lighter weight wrap since it is not lined.

MEXICAN BLANKET PONCHO

The typical Mexican poncho is made from a handwoven blanket and requires very little sewing. It is long, loose, and warm.

MATERIAL REQUIRED

1 woolen blanket (twin size) or 1⅓ yards of 60″ wide woolen fabric

CUTTING DIAGRAM

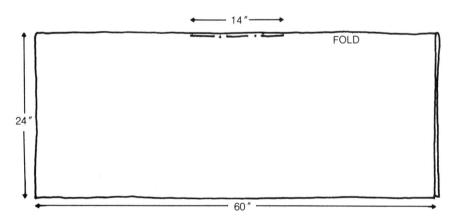

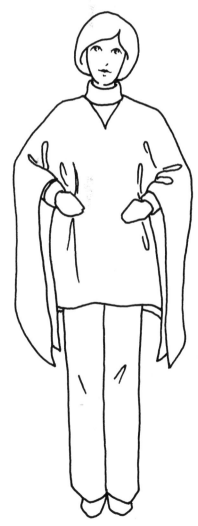

Fold the fabric in half the long way and cut a 14″ slit along the center of the fold. This slit forms the neck opening.

Finish the raw edge of the neckline by hemming with a zigzag stitch and/or crocheting or embroidering around it. If you have used a length of fabric rather than a blanket, finish the outer edges in the same way. Fringe may be added on each end or all around.

GREEK SHEEPHERDER'S JACKET

The Greek sheepherder's jacket is a handsome wrap for men or women and makes a lovely jacket for a child. Measurements can be changed easily to fit any size.

For a casual summer jacket use a denim type cotton. Wool, of course, makes a beautiful jacket that is warm and comfortable. Blanket wool is very nice and a handwoven fabric makes a jacket worthy of being an heirloom. Handweavers can easily weave the pieces to the correct dimensions in the first place so that no cutting is needed. Use matching or contrasting wool yarn to crochet all the pieces together; or join them with embroidery stitches. Handwoven striped cottons from Guatemala make particularly striking jackets. Use a strong color or black to crochet the garment together.

One of my favorite jackets was made from a piece of fabric from Italy—dark blue wool with a light turquoise stripe of mohair. I crocheted the pieces together with matching turquoise mohair yarn to make a wonderfully fuzzy looking warm jacket.

This design also can be made waist length with buttons down the front.

MATERIAL REQUIRED

> 1½ yards of 45″ wide fabric (average)
> 2 yards of 45″ wide fabric or 1⅔ yards of 54″ wide fabric (large)
> 1 yard of 45″ wide fabric (children's size)
> 1 4-oz. skein of 3-ply fingering yarn

CUTTING DIAGRAM

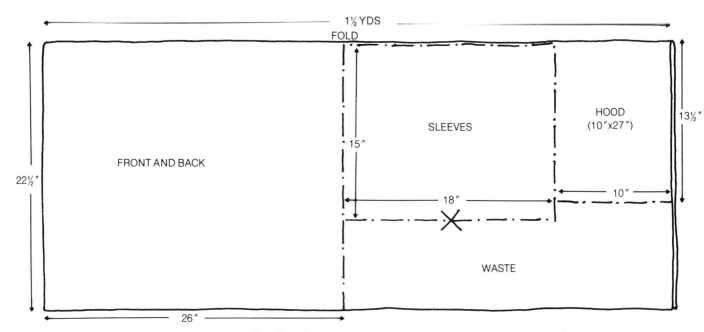

Cut the double 22½″ x 26″ piece into three pieces as follows:
 back—one piece 22″ x 26″
 front—two pieces 11½″ x 26″

Cut large size as follows:
 back—one piece 24″ x 30″
 front—two pieces 13″ x 30″
 sleeves—two pieces 20″ x 18″
 hood—one piece 12″ x 25″

Cut children's size as follows:
 back—one piece 20″ x 20″
 front—two pieces 10″ x 20″
 sleeves—two pieces 16″ x 14″
 hood—one piece 11½″ x 18″

METHOD OF CONSTRUCTION

Machine sew a zigzag stitch around each piece using matching thread.

Working from the right side of the fabric crochet one row alternating one single crochet and one chain stitch around each piece. Increase as needed at the corners. Repeat all around, again making several single crochet stitches in one hole at the corners to keep the fabric from buckling.

Starting at the shoulders place front to back, right sides out, with the back slightly higher than the front. Pin in place for 7" from the outside edge of the shoulder towards the neck. Beginning at the shoulder edge crochet back and forth between front and back three chain stitches between every third single crochet worked into the cloth (figure 1). Continue this for 7" leaving 4" from the shoulder to the middle of the neck in back, and 4½" from the shoulder to the middle of the front opening.

Figure 1

Match point X of the sleeve edge (see cutting diagram) to the crocheted shoulder seam and pin the sleeve in place. At this point check and align the sleeve and side seams and, if necessary, readjust the sleeve so one side will not be longer than the other. Again place the back slightly higher than the front so the work can be done more easily. Join the sleeves to the body using the same three chain stitches back and forth as you did the shoulder.

Work the underarm sleeve seams and side seams of the body the same way in one operation, leaving a 3" opening at the bottom of the jacket and if you like a 2½" opening at the bottom of the sleeve.

Fold the hood piece in half and crochet the 13½" seam up the back of the hood using the same three chain stitches.

Find the middle of the neck in the back and match the crocheted seam of the hood to this point. Pin the hood to the neckline all the way around to the front openings and crochet together in the same way (figure 2).

Crochet an edging using single crochet stitches with a picot stitch every fifth or sixth stitch or shell stitches around the sleeve edges. Do the same thing around the bottom edges of the jacket, and up the side and front openings and around the front of the hood.

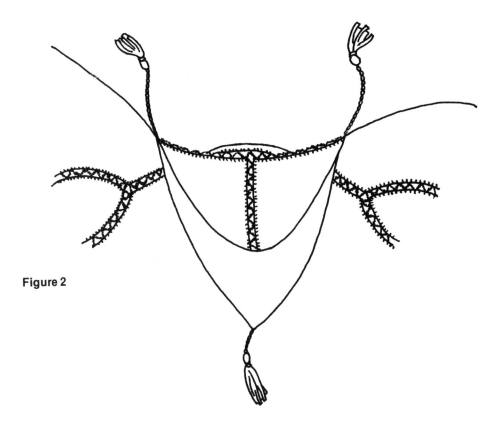

Figure 2

Crochet a 2″ chain at the point of the hood and attach a tassel.

Crochet a 22″ chain and run it through the crochet seam at the neckline. Attach tassels at the ends of the chain to tie at the neck. You may want to add one or two more sets of ties and tassels down the front to close the jacket at several points.

You may sew all pieces together with a needle and yarn instead of crochet if you wish. Figure 3 shows a suggested type of stitch to use.

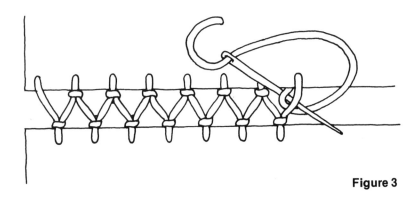

Figure 3

PORTUGUESE CAPE

Made of soft wool or one of the synthetic fabrics that drapes well, this cape has an elegant flare and swings jauntily as you walk. It is a wrap you can wear over sports clothes or evening clothes. Just slide your arms through the armhole slits, pull the back up against your neck, and you're ready for any occasion.

MATERIAL REQUIRED

2½ yards of 45″ wide fabric (wool or polyester jersey makes a beautiful cape)

2½ yards of 45″ wide lining fabric (for warmth, use material of the same weight as the outer fabric—in plaid, print, or a contrasting color; for a dressier cape, use lightweight jersey or some other soft, silky fabric)

½ yard of Pellon

CUTTING DIAGRAM

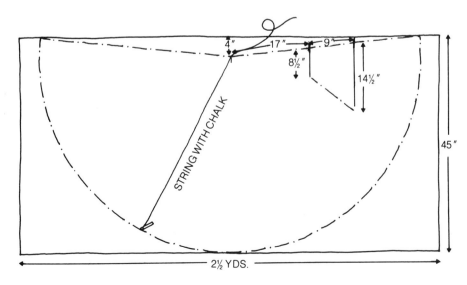

Place the fabric flat on the floor, find the center of the top edge, measure down 4″ and mark this point A. Take a string 45″ long, tie a piece of tailor's chalk to one end, and place the other end at point A on the fabric.

Starting with the chalk end of the string at the upper right corner of the fabric, bring the string down and around in a clockwise direction, pressing the chalk against the fabric as you do so to mark a semicircle. With chalk mark a straight line from point A to the upper right and left corners of the fabric, then cut out along the chalk lines all around.

From point A measure 17″ along the upper edge of the fabric, then down 8½″, and mark with a pin or tailor's chalk. Along the upper edge measure another 9″, then down 14½″, and mark that point. Cut a slit between those two points (see figure 1). Fold the fabric in half to mark the placement of the slit on the other side.

Cut the lining exactly as you cut the outer fabric.

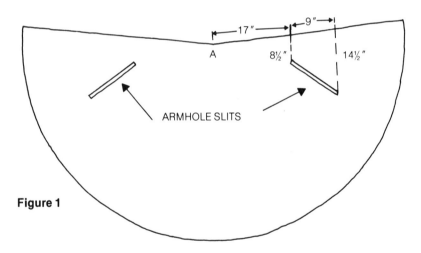

ARMHOLE SLITS

Figure 1

METHOD OF CONSTRUCTION

On the wrong side of the cape inner-face the armhole slits with strips of Pellon. Turn in the raw edges over the Pellon and baste in place.

Place the lining and cape together, right sides in, pin in place and machine sew a ½″ seam all around except for approximately 18″ at the bottom of the back to turn the garment right side out. Press and close the opening at the bottom with whip stitches.

Turn in the raw edges of the lining around the armhole slits and whip stitch in place. Top stitch by machine twice around the armhole slits to strengthen them.

MEXICAN QUESQUEMITL

A peasant shawl, also called *mañanita* (little morning), made from two fringed pieces of wool or heavy cotton is great to warm your shoulders against the early morning chill. Of course, it is equally cozy and attractive in midafternoon or late evening. Choose fabric that looks handwoven or, if you have a loom, weave your own lengths.

MATERIAL REQUIRED

    5/6 yard of 36″ wide fabric, or ½ yard of 60″ fabric
    2 yards of fringe
    (or use two fringed stoles approximately 30″ x 15″ each)

CUTTING DIAGRAM

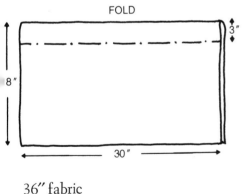

36″ fabric

60″ fabric

METHOD OF CONSTRUCTION

Hem all edges of the two pieces by machine using zigzag stitches. Then trim the four ends with fringe. Add tassels to the corners if you wish.

Figure 1

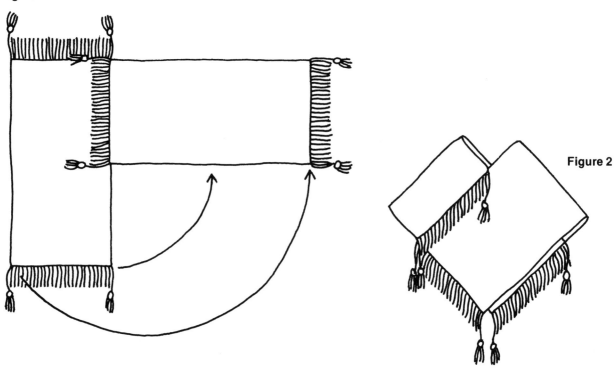

Figure 2

Join the two pieces as shown in figure 1, sewing them together from the underside. The fringe then accents the middle and one side of the front and back (figure 2). You may add fringe to the untrimmed edges in front and back if you prefer a more symmetrical look.

Many boutiques now carry readymade quesquemitls but they are so easy to make that it hardly pays to buy them. And when you make one in a fabric of your choice, trimmed with unusual fringe, embroidery, or braid, you have a completely distinctive wrap.

GYPSY
FOUR-WAY CAPE

This is a dramatic garment that adapts itself to your every mood. It looks dashing when thrown over gaucho pants and vest during the day, and exotic when worn over a long ruffled skirt and peasant blouse in the evening. Worn in its shortest version with simulated collar and lapels, fastened Scottish style with a large heraldic pin, it has a tailored air. The top fold pulls up over your head to protect your hair from wind or rain. Since this one cape can be worn in four different lengths it will look wonderful over almost everything in your wardrobe—the perfect wrap for making grand entrances.

Choose a wool fabric that falls gracefully and folds easily. Select a wool that is equally attractive on both sides. I made this cape out of an old navy blanket—gray with specks of red and blue in the weave. It is warm, soft, and manageable, and when I am traveling it serves as an extra blanket when needed.

MATERIAL REQUIRED

    1⅔ yards of 54″ wide fabric—average size oval cape
      or 1½ yards of 54″ wide fabric—small size round cape
      or 1⅔ yards of 60″ wide fabric—large size round cape
  4 2-oz. skeins of yarn

Fold the fabric in half lengthwise, then fold it in half again across the width. Using a tape measure or string to guide you, mark the outer cutting edge with tailor's chalk as shown in figure 1. Be careful not to start the curve abruptly at point A or end it abruptly at point B; cut almost parallel to the edge of the fabric for the first and last few inches to make a smooth curve all around. (You may want to try it first on a smaller scale using paper.) Without unfolding the fabric, cut along the marked line—two layers at a time since it is difficult to cut through four thicknesses of fabric at one time.

Unfold the fabric once, leaving it folded in half lengthwise as shown in figure 2. Measure down 20″ along the fold and mark this point C. Measure perpendicularly from point C a distance equal to half the width of your shoulders and mark this point D. Measure straight down 11″ and mark this point E; then cut a slit between points D and E in the top layer of fabric. Mark the underneath layer of fabric to match and cut a second slit. When unfolded the fabric will look as shown in figure 3.

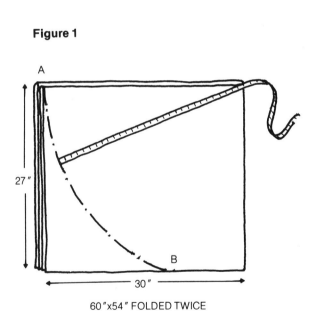

Figure 1

27″

30″

60″x54″ FOLDED TWICE

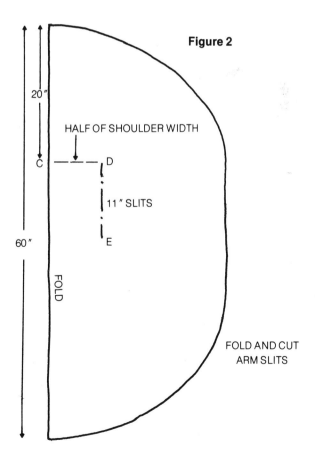

Figure 2

20″

HALF OF SHOULDER WIDTH

11″ SLITS

60″

FOLD

FOLD AND CUT
ARM SLITS

Figure 3

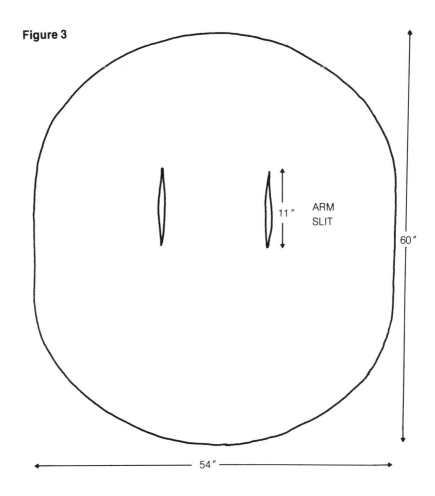

11″ ARM SLIT

60″

54″

METHOD OF CONSTRUCTION

Machine sew around the outer edge of the cape and around the arm slits using a zigzag or straight stitch. Then crochet one row of alternating single crochet and chain stitches around each slit and all around the cape. The single row finishes the slits.

Add a second row of crochet around the cape, alternating one double crochet and three chain stitches, anchoring the double stitches in between every other single crochet of the first row. If the work begins to buckle add an extra stitch to the three chain stitches for several spaces and proceed as before.

When you have finished the second row make the tassel fringe. Cut a strip of cardboard about ½″ longer than you want your tassel fringe to be. To make a single tassel wrap a piece of yarn around the cardboard three times. Cut the ends at the bottom, pinching the top together into a loop. Place the loop against the edge of the cape and with a crochet hook pull the loop through one of the spaces in the double crochet row, then slide the ends through the loop and pull tight to anchor the tassel. Repeat this all the way around the cape (figure 4).

1 SINGLE CROCHET, 1 CHAIN STITCH

DOUBLE CROCHET SPACES

Figure 4

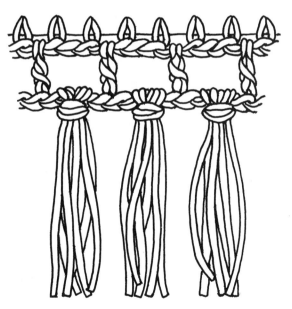

TASSEL FRINGE ADDED

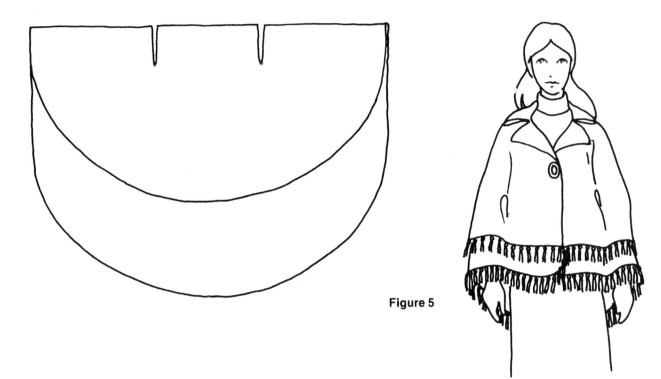

Figure 5

FOUR WAYS TO WEAR THE GYPSY CAPE

Fold the cape over at the point where the slits will form collar and lapels, throw it across your shoulders, and wrap to the front. This makes the short Scottish cape to fasten with a broach (figure 5).

With the circle open and the shorter length of the cape at the top, slip your arms through the slits and draw the upper part of the cape closely around your neck, wrapped to the front. This makes the long version (figure 6).

With the circle open and the longer end of the cape at the top, slip your arms through the slits and wrap to the front for a shorter version (figure 7).

To make a face-framing hood, drape the upper part of the cape over your head as shown in figure 8.

Figure 6

Figure 7

Figure 8

Tops

MEXICAN JUIPIL

The juipil is extremely simple to make and very becoming—particularly when made of soft handwoven fabric.

MATERIAL REQUIRED

2 scarves each approximately 40″ to 45″ long, 12″ wide or ⅔ yard of 45″ wide fabric

If you are using two scarves place one on top of the other (figure 1), right sides in. Starting at the bottom edge, machine sew up to point A (8″ below center). Do the same from the top edge to point B. This leaves a 16″ slit for the neckline. Make the opening longer if you prefer a lower neckline. Attach front to back underarms with tasseled ties or machine stitch for 2″ or 3″; or put in grommets and lace with a cord or leather thong (figure 2).

You can also use a rectangle of fabric with a slit vertically in the middle for the neckline. Finish the slit by hand with buttonhole stitches or by machine with a zigzag stitch.

This is very comfortable to wear in warm weather with a skirt or pants. Made of wool for cooler climates it is nice to wear over a long-sleeved turtleneck shirt and pants. Made of terry-cloth, lace, or cotton print it is fun to wear over swim suits. You may also want to make a longer tunic-length version of the juipil.

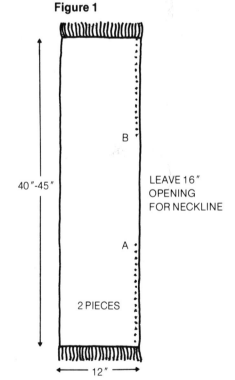

Figure 1

40″-45″

B

A

2 PIECES

LEAVE 16″ OPENING FOR NECKLINE

12″

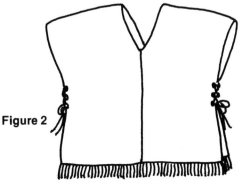

Figure 2

JAPANESE KAPOGI

The Kapogi apron is a Japanese design traditionally made of white or pastel colored cotton, trimmed with embroidery edging. It has elbow length sleeves with elastic at the bottom so they can be pushed up. This adaptation is made of bright sturdy cotton and uses a contrasting print cotton for the sleeves, neck openings, ties, and pockets. Polished cotton with a corresponding flowered polished cotton for the sleeves makes a beautiful gift apron. It also can be made of ripply nylon or striped seersucker that does not require ironing.

The apron is becoming as well as practical and fits any size except very large (directions for which are also included in the following diagrams). It has a smock-like appearance and is a great cover-up because it goes all around the body. I have made kapogis for artists to wear when they paint. If you prefer you can make the bottom of the apron straight all around and stitch up the back leaving a neck opening and ties at the top of the back, and wear it as a dress or top for pants.

I suggest you use the cutting directions for making a paper pattern first as you probably will want to make several of these attractive aprons. I have many paper patterns I have cut from these diagrams and then filed in cellophane bags with a picture or description inside so I can readily pull the one I want out of my collection and cut it quickly when I am in a hurry.

MATERIAL REQUIRED

1 yard of 45″ wide fabric (solid color)
½ yard of 45″ wide fabric (print)

CUTTING DIAGRAM

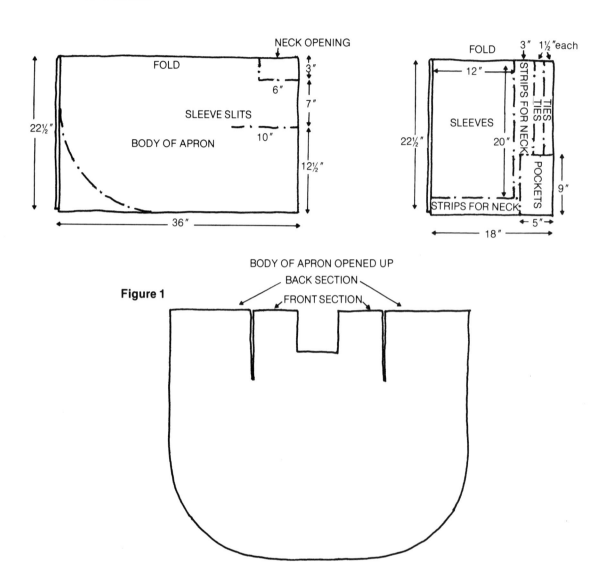

Figure 1

To make this apron smaller use 36″ wide fabric instead of 45″ wide. To make it very large buy a yard of contrasting fabric instead of ½ yard, and add a 3″ or 4″ wide panel of the contrasting fabric right down the middle of the apron. Do this before you cut the neckline and sleeve slits. Make the sleeves 2″ wider. You can cut the apron longer or shorter in length as you wish. If longer, you will need an extra ½ yard or so of material.

The leftover pieces of print fabric can be used for the sleeves, ties, etc. of other aprons. Using a different print for each contrasting part, and adding rickrack or braid trim to tie it all together, can be very attractive.

METHOD OF CONSTRUCTION

Neck

Open up the body of the apron to the wrong side of the fabric (figure 1). Pin an 8″ strip of the neck facing right side down—right side to the wrong side. When the seam is made and the strip is turned over, the right side will be on the outside of the kapogi, forming a decorative facing. Sew the facing in place with a ⅝″ seam (figure 2). Clip the corner and turn the facing to the right side. Press it flat, turn under the edges and top stitch in place (figure 3). Sew the other strip on the other side in the same fashion.

Cut a 2½″ x 10″ strip and pin it to the wrong side of the bottom edge of the neck, aligning the middle of the strip with the middle of the neck edge (figure 4). Sew, clip and turn. Press and turn under all raw edges. This will overlay the ends of the 9″ strips sewn on the sides of the neck. Turn under each end in an arrow shape and top stitch in place (figure 5). I also top stitch the seamed edges for a neat finish.

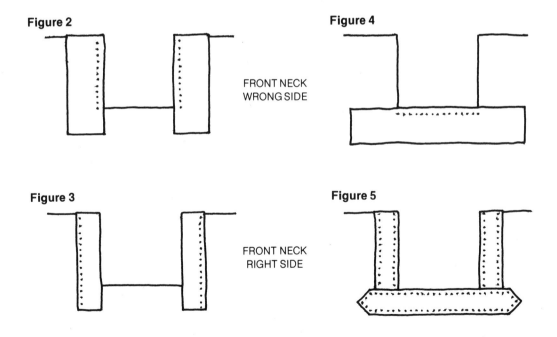

Figure 2

Figure 4

FRONT NECK
WRONG SIDE

Figure 3

Figure 5

FRONT NECK
RIGHT SIDE

Ties

Cut the tie pieces in half along the fold to make four pieces, each 13½" x 1½". Fold right side in, stitch down the side and across one end of each tie (figure 6) and turn right side out by pushing through the closed end using a chopstick or a pencil.

Shoulder Seams

Turn the apron to the wrong side and align the sleeve slits. Pin the front section to the back section at the top edges with right sides together. Machine sew a 1½" shoulder seam from the sleeve slit to the neck opening on each side (see figure 7). Then hem the balance of the shoulder edge on either side (from neck opening to center back opening) so there are no raw edges along the shoulder line.

Figure 6

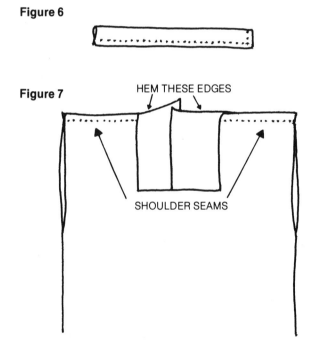

Figure 7

HEM THESE EDGES

SHOULDER SEAMS

Sleeves

Fold one sleeve section in half, right side in. Sew the underarm seam and hem one edge (figure 8). Press. Turn right side out.

Turn the apron wrong side out. Slip the sleeve into the slit, aligning the raw edges of sleeve and apron sleeve slit and

Figure 8

Figure 9

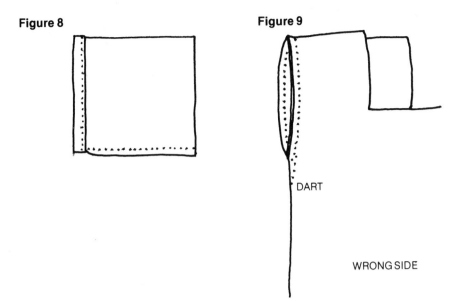

DART

WRONG SIDE

the underarm seam with the bottom of the slit (figure 9). Pin in place and sew a ½″ seam all around the armhole. Make a small dart from where the underarm seam ends to 1½″ below the seam for a smooth underarm effect. Repeat with the second sleeve.

Mark with a pin on each side of the back opening where the neckline and waist ties should be. Hem all around the apron attaching the ties to the hem as you sew (figure 10). You may make one large pocket in the center front or two pockets, one on each side. Press and the apron is ready to wear or wrap up for a gift. You should be able to make one in an hour and a half including the cutting time.

Figure 10

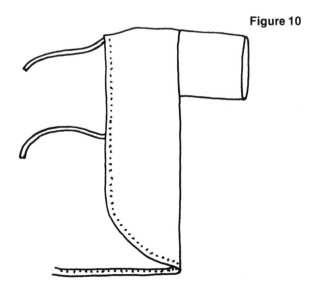

Also included is a cutting diagram for the original Japanese style kapogi. Make this of soft cotton, trim with lace or ruffles, and run elastic through the hem of the sleeve. A ruffle around the bottom makes a frothy pinafore type of apron.

MATERIAL REQUIRED

    1½ yards 36″ fabric
    1 yard embroidery trim
    1 yard lace or ruffle trim   } (to face and trim neck)

CUTTING DIAGRAM

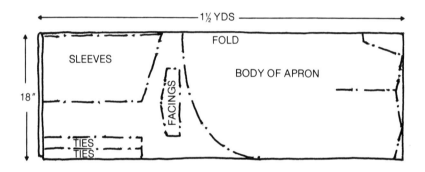

LULU

Lulu is my own name for this loose, comfortable peasant top. It looks equally well with a skirt or pants, worn straight or cinched in with a leather, macrame, or handwoven belt.

MATERIAL REQUIRED

1⅓ yards of 45″ wide fabric
embroidery yarn

CUTTING DIAGRAM

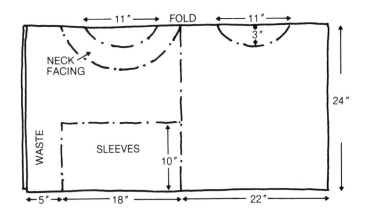

Neck opening: 11″ across, 3″ deep at center
Neck facing: same dimensions as neck opening at inner
curve, 2½″ deeper at outer curve

METHOD OF CONSTRUCTION

First face the neckline. Place the right side of the facing against the right side of the garment and pin in place. Machine sew around the neckline ½″ in from the edge. At several points

around the neckline clip in just short of the stitching so the curves will lie flat. Turn the facing in to the wrong side and hem or machine sew a zigzag stitch along the raw edge. Then anchor the facing to the garment with a tack stitch here and there.

Next place the center of one of the sleeves (point X) right side down against the right side of the shoulder fold (figure 1). Pin in place and machine sew the sleeve to the body of the garment. Attach the second sleeve in the same way.

Now fold the garment in half at the shoulder line, wrong sides out. Make the right underarm seam starting at the outer edge of the sleeve and stitching to within 1½″ of the armhole. Make the left underarm seam in the same way.

Figure 1

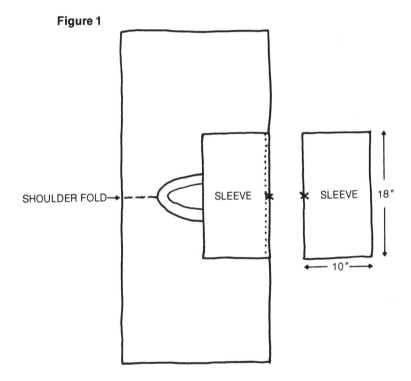

To make the side seams start at the bottom edge of the blouse and stitch up to within 1½″ of the armhole on either side (figure 2). This leaves a diamond shape opening where the sleeve joins the body. Hem the raw edges of the openings. These underarm openings are characteristic of many peasant garments. They not only prevent the garment from tearing at a stress point, but provide ventilation and make the garment easy to fold flat for storing in a chest or drawer.

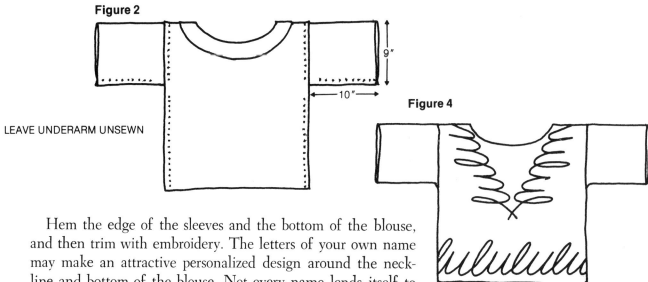

Figure 2

9"

←—10"—→

LEAVE UNDERARM UNSEWN

Figure 4

Hem the edge of the sleeves and the bottom of the blouse, and then trim with embroidery. The letters of your own name may make an attractive personalized design around the neckline and bottom of the blouse. Not every name lends itself to a curvilinear pattern, but most three to five letter names work well (figure 3). Develop the design on paper first, transfer it to the fabric, and then embroider it using chain or outline stitches (figure 4).

To make an interesting variation of the lulu, use two different color fabrics, and applique a scroll design down the front (see figure 5).

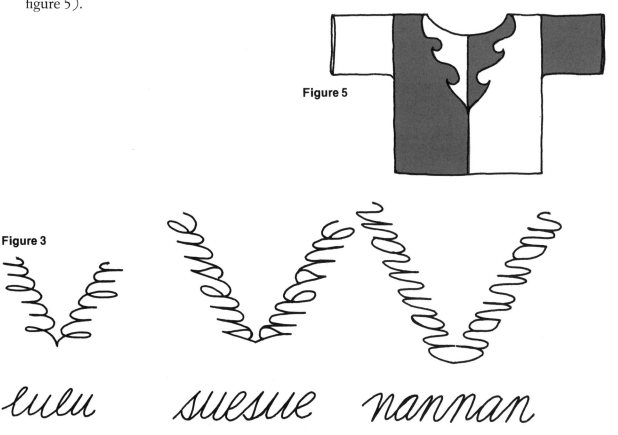

Figure 5

Figure 3

lulu   *suesue*   *nannan*

RUANA

A ruana is a flattering cape-like garment. It is comfortable to wear because it stays in place well, whether you cross the ends in front, toss one end over your shoulder, or drape it in some other fashion. Some of the most beautiful ruanas are imported from Ecuador, Colombia and Peru—warm, double woven wool in brilliant colors with fringes at the bottom of the front and back. To make an authentic looking ruana use alpaca or llama wool fringed all around with combed lamb or goat wool.

This wrap looks handsome in almost any kind of wool. If you prefer a sleek rather than a bulky look, use wool jersey lined with another color of the same fabric. A crocheted edging around a heavier material creates a looped, puffy look which is also appealing. A ruana made of white wool lined with satin and trimmed with maribou is an elegant evening wrap.

MATERIAL REQUIRED

⅔ yard of 54″ wide outer fabric
⅔ yard of 54″ wide lining fabric (optional)
6 yards of fringe (optional, other trimming may be sub-stituted)

CUTTING DIAGRAM

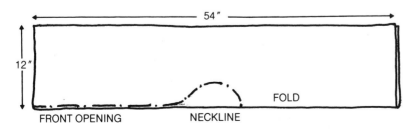

METHOD OF CONSTRUCTION

Cut halfway along the length of the fold to make the front opening, curving in slightly to form a rounded neckline, as shown in the cutting diagram. If you are not lining the ruana, machine sew a zigzag stitch around all the edges and add fringe or a crocheted edging.

To make a lined ruana, cut the lining exactly the same as the outer fabric. Place both pieces of fabric together, right sides in, and machine stitch them together around the outer edges, leaving the front opening and neckline open. Turn right side out, press, turn in the raw edges of the front opening and neckline and whip stitch in place. Then trim with fringe or crochet.

CROCHET–TOGETHER
PEASANT SHIRT

If you enjoy crocheting, this shirt is very simple to make and a beauty to wear. It looks marvelous worn unbelted with pants, or belted with a skirt and boots. You only need to know how to chain stitch, single crochet, and double crochet, and the only sewing required is a zigzag stitch around all pieces to prevent raveling.

The secret of this garment is using just the right fabric. I found a cotton imported from Holland with a bold, colorful geometric African type design. It looks handwoven and has the appearance and feel of wool. This makes an excellent fabric for the pattern. Whenever I wear my red/gray shirt with gray slacks and a black long-sleeved turtleneck underneath I always get orders for another one.

Of course, you may find other materials that please you. You can even recycle an older garment where the fabric is not worn and cut your pieces from that. I have even used strips of fabric crocheted together to make the body and sleeves of the shirt. I once used strips left over from striped velvet upholstery fabric in beautiful shades of dark red and crocheted it together with black yarn. You can let your imagination run rampant in these types of combinations. Diagrams and measurements for these adaptations are given at the end of this chapter.

MATERIAL REQUIRED

    1 yard 45″ wide fabric (1½ yard 54″ fabric for large size)
    1 4-oz. skein 3-ply fingering yarn
    4 small buttons

CUTTING DIAGRAM I

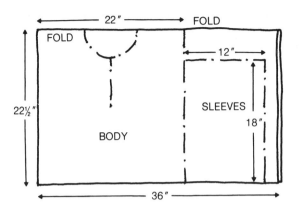

1 yard 45″ fabric

Medium size: (cut as above)
    body 22″ x 22½″
    sleeve 18″ x 12″

Small size: (adjust above dimensions)
    body 20″ x 22½″
    sleeve 16″ x 10″

CUTTING DIAGRAM II

1½ yards 54″ fabric
Large size:
    body 25″ x 27″
    sleeve 20″ x 14½″

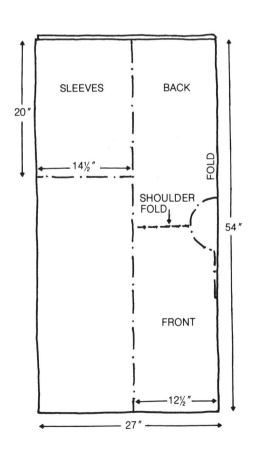

METHOD OF CONSTRUCTION

First zigzag with your sewing machine around each piece to prevent the fabric from raveling and to give a stronger edge for the crochet stitches.

To crochet

Start with a slip knot in wool yarn and from the right side of the garment make a row of single crochet completely around each piece, being sure to increase at the corners by one chain stitch between each single crochet done in one hole at each corner. After completing the first row of single crochet chain three, turn and double crochet a second row completely around each piece; and again at the corners, do an extra double crochet, twice in the same hole, to increase for the curve and keep the piece flat.

Before joining the pieces together crochet around the neck and front opening slit as it will be easier to do before the garment is assembled.

Neck opening and slit

Working with the fabric right side up begin at the bottom right edge of the 7″ slit opening and single crochet one row all the way around to the bottom of the left edge opening.

Then chain three stitches, turn and double crochet a second row completely around to the bottom right side of the opening.

Chain 1 and turn, then do single crochet up the right side for five stitches, chain 3 and single crochet in the third double crochet from the start of the chain to make a buttonhole. Repeat this procedure until you reach the top of the right side.

Increase to ease the corner and single crochet around the neck, down the left side of the slit, across the lap and start up the right side of the slit doing 5 or 8 single crochet, chain 3 and single crochet in same hole to make a picot; proceed up the right opening, around the neck and plain single crochet down the left side opening. Tack the lap at the bottom of the opening using a needle and yarn.

Placing right sides together securely pin the edge of the sleeve to the shirt body, placing the center of sleeve edge A to the shoulder fold line A on the body piece (figures 1a and 1b). Crochet together on the wrong side with a single crochet stitch done rather loosely to prevent the finished garment from buckling.

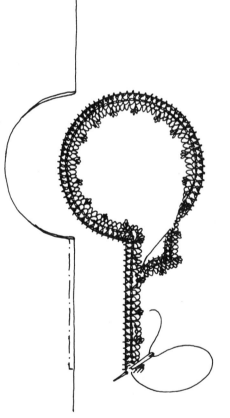

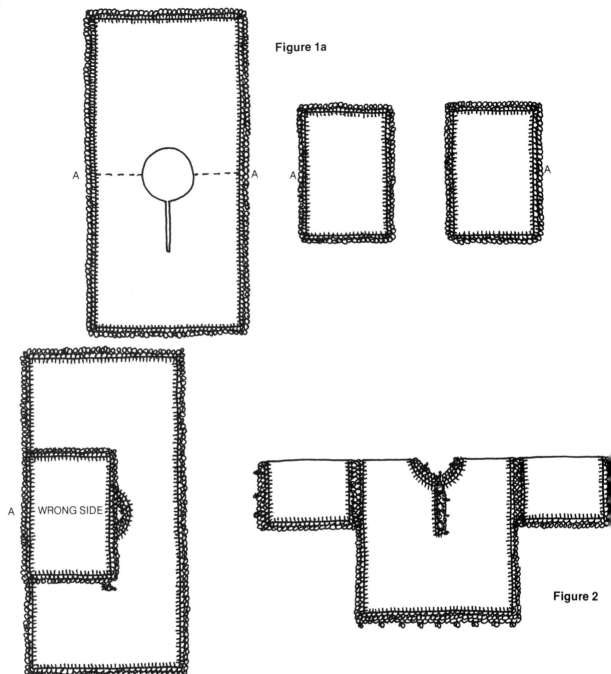

Figure 1a

Figure 1b

A → WRONG SIDE

Figure 2

Attach the other sleeve in the same way.

Turn the garment to the wrong side and pin together securely. Join the underarm and side seams together, using a loose single crochet stitch (figure 2).

Then turn the shirt right side out and make a row of double crochet around the edge of each sleeve and around the bottom of the shirt. Complete the edging with a row of single crochet with a picot every 5 or 8 stitches. Sew buttons on the neck opening opposite the crocheted buttonholes.

The finished garment should be at least 2″ or 3″ (including crochet) larger around than your hip or thigh measurement.

ADAPTATIONS

To make a shirt out of strips you will need the following:

2—5″ x 40″ side strips
4—5″ x 18″ front and back strips
4—5″ x 16″ sleeve strips

If the fabric is coarse you may want to line the strips first. Crochet around each strip with two rows of double crochet, then join the strips on the back side as shown in figure 3 with a loose single crochet stitch. Crochet an edging around the neck, sleeves, and bottom of the shirt after the strips are crocheted together (figure 4).

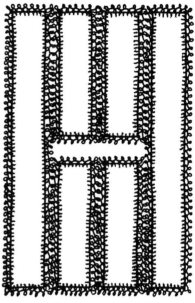

Figure 3

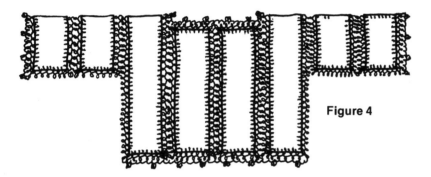

Figure 4

Another adaptation and the simplest to make is done with two body pieces cut 19″ x 20″ and the sleeve pieces cut 16″ x 12″. (If your hips measure more than 36″ around, and if you want the blouse to be longer, cut the body pieces 20″ wide x 26″ long.) These pieces are crocheted all around with two rows of double crochet, increasing as needed at the corners, then joined on the wrong side with single crochet. Be sure to pin the pieces together securely before starting so that all the edges are aligned evenly. The shoulder seam is crocheted together leaving a 12″ opening for the neck. Make a single crochet and picot edging around neck or whatever edging you prefer, using the same around the sleeves and bottom of the shirt (figure 5).

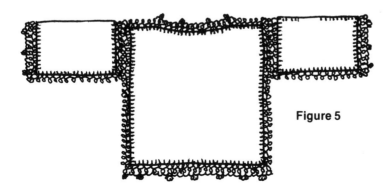

Figure 5

MEXICAN EMBROIDERED BLOUSE

This design from Mexico is marvelous to wear in hot climates because the back falls free to catch every breeze. Heavy embroidery decorates the neckline and armholes. The original version of this blouse is sometimes as wide around as 68″ and all the fullness is tucked into a full skirt. This is a bit bulky for most tastes, so I have reduced the fullness somewhat.

Use soft cotton or a lovely sheer fabric such as voile, trimmed with embroidery in gay, bright colors. Or you might consider using a solid color East Indian bedspread. East Indian cotton crepe also makes a lovely blouse, but the fabric must be laundered first as there is shrinkage.

If you do not want to do all the handwork you can use a print fabric to face the neck and armholes and trim with an embroidered edging.

MATERIAL REQUIRED

> 1¼ yards of 45″ wide fabric (if using same fabric for facing), or ¾ yard of 45″ wide solid color fabric (for blouse) plus ½ yard of 36″ wide print fabric (for facings)

CUTTING DIAGRAM

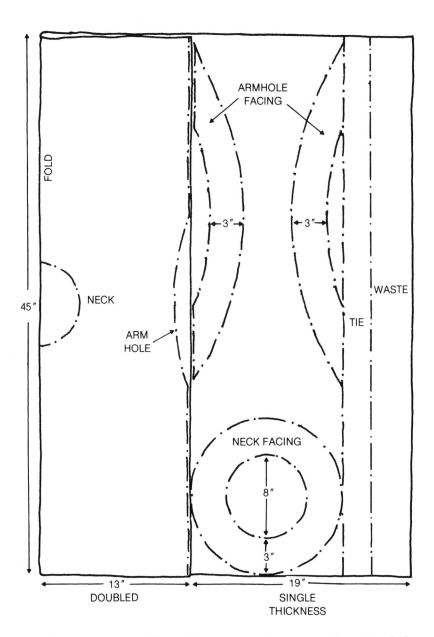

As you can see from the cutting diagram, only 26″ of the fabric is folded in half to make a doubled piece 45″ x 13″, from which the blouse is cut. The facings and tie are cut from the remaining single piece measuring 45″ x 19″. Using pins or tailor's chalk, mark the 8″ diameter neckline curve and the armhole curve, which should be approximately 15″ long and 1½″ deep at the shoulder line (figure 1).

Figure 1

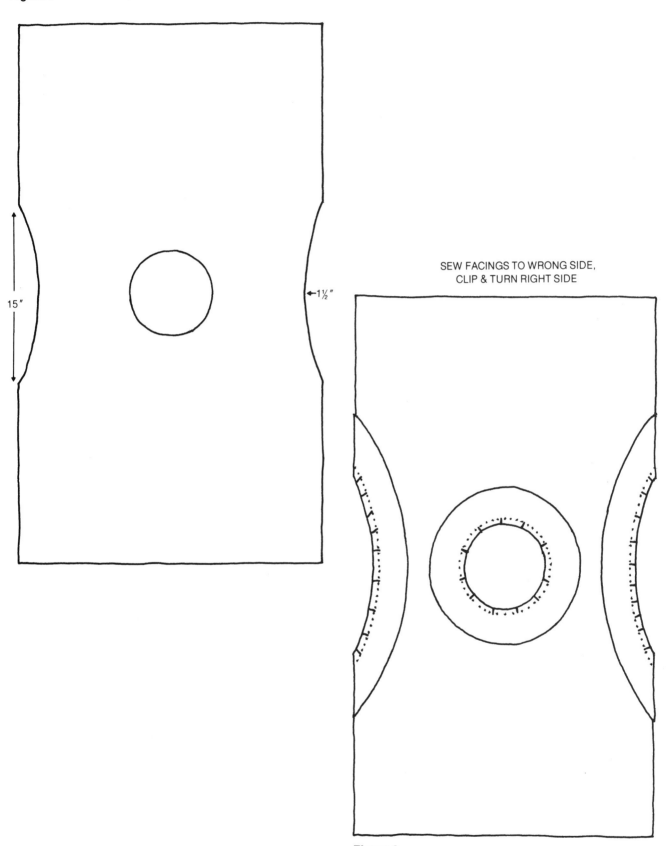

15″

←1½″

SEW FACINGS TO WRONG SIDE,
CLIP & TURN RIGHT SIDE

Figure 2

Figure 3

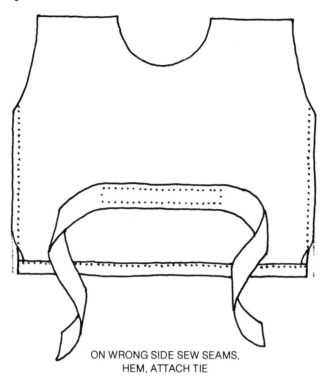

ON WRONG SIDE SEW SEAMS,
HEM, ATTACH TIE

Use the pieces cut out for the neckline and armholes to measure and mark the facings, which should be 3″ deep. Trim the facings with embroidery before attaching them to the neckline and armholes. It is much easier to work on these small pieces separately than on the completed garment.

Be sure to leave a ½″ seam allowance on the facings for attaching them to the neck and armhole edges and turning under the raw edges when you sew the facings to the front of the garment.

METHOD OF CONSTRUCTION

Place the armhole and neck facings right side down against the wrong side of the blouse. Pin in place and stitch a ½″ seam at the neck and armhole edges. Clip the curves just short of the seams so the curves will lie flat (figure 2). Turn right side out and press. Turn under the raw edges of the facings and join them to the body of the blouse using embroidery stitches—buttonhole or any other edging stitch you particularly like, adding an additional row or two of border embroidery on the body of the blouse.

Turn the blouse inside out again, align the side seams, pin, and stitch together by machine. Then make a 1″ hem at the bottom of the blouse.

Before turning the blouse right side out, hem the tie strip by machine (you may substitute 1½ yards of cotton tape for this strip) and stitch about 10″ of the center of the tie to the front of the blouse at the waistline, on the wrong side (figure 3). The ends remain free to tie in back under the blouse; the front hugs the body while the sides and back float free (figure 4).

This design can be made any length you like—to the knee, mid-calf, or floor length. If you make it as a dress, add a border of embroidery around the bottom.

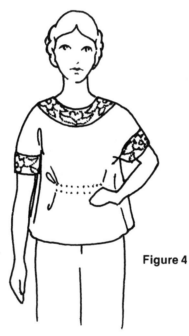

Figure 4

Accessories

MAD CAP

The mad cap is an adaptation of the old-fashioned maid's duster cap. It is great to wear in an open car or over curlers when you run out to shop. Made of burlap lined with cotton and trimmed with yarn around the brim and bright beads at the ends of the ties it protects your hair from wind and sun. Made of clear plastic it is a great rain hat. Bind the edges with grosgrain ribbon and tie on a jaunty bow. Embroidered cotton, lace or a sheer nylon net make this an unusual quaint bridesmaid's hat. Adorn it with velvet ribbons or flowers to match the gown.

For a child's bonnet, make it of double organdy. Pink the edges of the brim and attach small sprigs of flowers on each side with ribbon ties to go under the chin. Measurements for a child's mad cap should be 34″ x 12½″.

MATERIAL REQUIRED

½ yard 45″ wide burlap or linen-like fabric
½ yard 45″ wide for lining or
    ½ yard 45″ wide plastic and 2½ yards grosgrain ribbon
    (for rainhat)
¾ yard of ⅜″ elastic
Yarn, beads, bells, flowers, ribbon or whatever you wish
    for trim

CUTTING DIAGRAMS (SAME FOR CAP AND LINING)

Measurements for child's version: 34" x 12½"

18"

40"   5"

WASTE

METHOD OF CONSTRUCTION

Fold the cap fabric in half, right side in, and machine sew the ends together to make a continuous circle (figure 1). Do exactly the same with the lining. Press the seams open. Align the seams of the cap and lining and with right sides together, sew them together along one edge for the ruffled brim of that hat (figure 2). Turn right side out and press.

Measure up 5" from the sewn edge and mark with tailor's chalk all around. Machine sew along this line. Measure up ½" from this row of stitches and sew all around to make a casing for the elastic (figure 3). Make an opening in the lining seam between the casing stitches and insert elastic to fit the head comfortably. Sew elastic together by hand and resew the opening in the lining.

Turn the cap wrong side out, pinch both lining and outer fabric together in several 1½" pleats at the top (figure 4) and stitch through all pleat layers to hold them in place. Finish the raw edges and turn right side out. This makes a chic puffy top. Wrap yarn or ribbon loosely around the elasticized casing, tacking it to the cap in several places, making sure there is enough give to stretch the same as the elastic. Tie a bow and add bells or beads to the ends of the yarn or ribbon (figure 5). Or you can use a simple macrame cord to tie around the hat.

If you make the rainhat you will not need a lining—just bind the brim edge with grosgrain ribbon and attach a band of ribbon on the right side over the casing. Choose ribbon to match your raincoat.

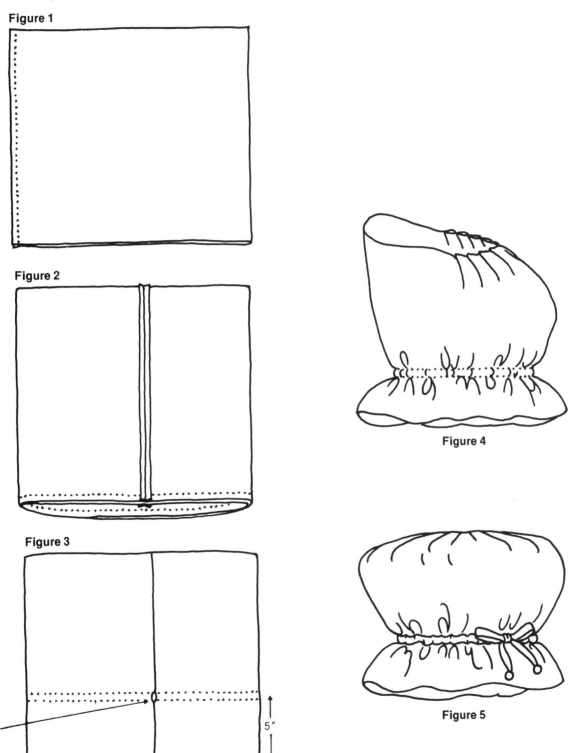

Figure 1

Figure 2

Figure 3

INSERT
ELASTIC

5"

Figure 4

Figure 5

ECUADORIAN
SADDLE BAG

This double pouch bag is as attractive as it is practical. Adapted from the earlier leather saddle bag that could be slung across the back of a horse or donkey, the modern fabric version is ideal for marketing or traveling. When shopping you can put wallet, keys, makeup, tissues, etc., in one pouch and keep the other free for stowing away a variety of small purchases. When traveling, it makes a handy carryall for those bulky, odd-shaped items that won't quite fit into the suitcase. For short trips I sometimes use it instead of a suitcase. With a toothbrush, makeup case, nightgown and slippers tucked into one side, sandals and a crush-proof jersey evening dress on the other side, and wearing a comfortable pants suit, I'm all set for a weekend away.

The peasant version of the saddle bag is generally made of multicolored cotton strips woven together in much the same way as rag rugs are, and decorated with strips of felt, braid, and embroidery. Good alternatives to the traditional handwoven fabric are canvas or sturdy drapery or upholstery fabric. Ideally the cloth should be identical on both sides, but if you fall in love with a patterned cloth that isn't reversible you can always use a doubled piece to make it so.

MATERIAL REQUIRED

> 13″ x 60″ piece of reversible fabric (27″ x 60″ if fabric has to be doubled)
> ¼ yard of felt
> 2 yards of double braid
> embroidery yarn, ball fringe, braid, tassels, etc. as desired for trim
> handle—wooden, metal, or plastic ring or semicircle with minimum 8″ diameter

METHOD OF CONSTRUCTION

Cut two felt strips each 13″ x 1½″. Fold these strips over the raw edges at either end of the 13″ x 60″ piece of fabric and sew firmly in place with embroidery stitches. I recommend overcast stitches going first in one direction across the entire width, and then back in the opposite direction, to give a criss-cross effect.

Two inches in from the felt edge machine sew a band of braid across the width. Another ¾″ in from the braid band sew a row of ball fringe. Be sure the fringe is placed so it will fall correctly when the fabric is folded up to form a pouch (see figures 1 and 2). Follow this row of fringe with several more rows of braid, embroidery, or whatever, varying the distance between each row in any way that is pleasing. Then repeat the same pattern at the other end, being certain the row of fringe falls in the opposite direction.

Then, with the decorative pattern facing out, fold up each end 12½″ and pin in place (see figure 2). Fold the double braid over the raw edges along the entire length of each side. If these multiple layers of fabric are too bulky to sew by machine, sew the braid on by hand with back stitches, using doubled heavy-duty thread. Add tassels at the bottom corners of both pouches.

To finish the bag, slip one end through the handle and position the fabric in equal lengths on either side of the ring or semicircle (see figure 3). Tack the fabric firmly in place under the handle, and the bag is ready to use or give as a gift.

Figure 1

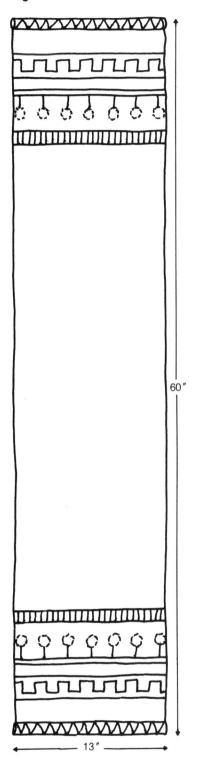

60″

13″

Figure 2

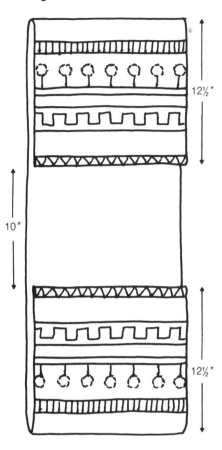

12½″

10″

12½″

Figure 3

Skirts, Dresses, Robes

BUTTERFLY
MUUMUU

The name of this garment is suggested by its shape. When opened out it resembles a butterfly. It is a graceful, comfortable, long dress suitable for casual or formal occasions depending on your choice of fabric. Made of velour or corduroy it can be a warm robe to wear over nightgown or pajamas while you prepare breakfast or relax in the evening by the fire. Made of cotton it can be a beach cover-up or a casual hostess dress. Use print corduroy for a cozy, warm winter at-home dress. Make it of silk, taffeta or velvet and it can be worn out to dinner or for your own special entertaining. The one loaned to me by a friend to draw and cut the pattern was made of silk taffeta from India with a border design of gold threads. One of my favorite fabrics to use for this design is a fine quality cotton bedspread from India with a hand printed border design, or a heavier grade cotton batik spread. Fabrics with bold border designs are especially effective for this pattern.

MATERIAL REQUIRED

    1 twin bedspread approximately 74″ x 112″ or
    2⅞ yards of 45″ wide fabric or
    2⅓ yards of 54″ wide fabric
  3½ yards of woven braid to match or contrast fabric colors
  1 spool of thread to match fabric

You will need fabric long enough to cut twice your length from shoulder to hemline plus 1″ or 2″ to turn up for the hem. The border design is most effective when it circles the bottom of the skirt. Leave just enough fabric at the lower edge for the hem—be certain not to turn under any of the border design.

CUTTING DIAGRAM

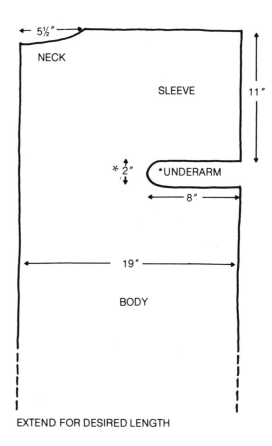

Small:
  neck the same
  17″ wide
  sleeve 9″
  curve underarm 9″ x 2″

Medium:
  as diagrammed

Large:
  neck the same
  20″ wide
  sleeve 12″
  curve underarm 8″ x 3″ or 4″

*If your bustline is heavy and low you should make the depth of the underarm cut 4″ instead of 3″ so the ties will fit easily under the bust for an empire effect.

Fabric layout for twin-sized bedspread border print design

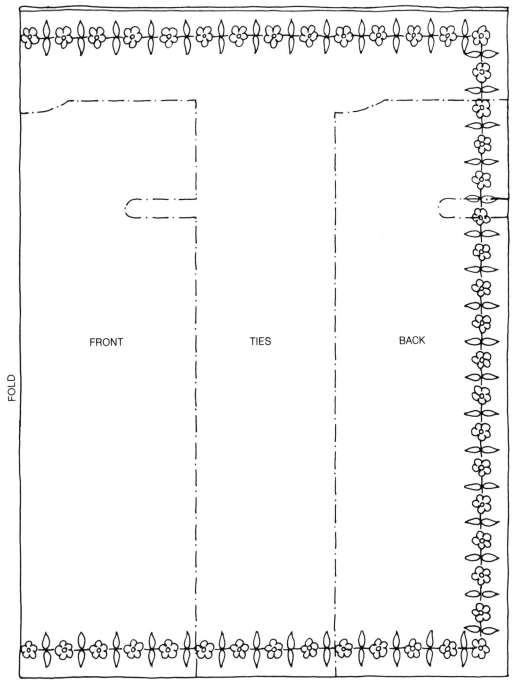

FOLD

FRONT   TIES   BACK

CUTTING INSTRUCTIONS

When using an Indian bedspread fold it the wide way rather than the long way so as to have more width for the two body pieces. This will probably leave a seam across the middle of the garment, which is alright as it scarcely shows; using the border design effectively is a more important consideration. You may wish to resew this seam for greater strength.

When folding the spread be sure to align the border design and pin in place. Often India prints are not completely true so you may want to cut the body pieces separately using the border design as a guide to keep the edges aligned straight with the border.

You can mark the pattern directly on the fabric using straight pins or tailor's chalk. Or, preferably, you can measure and cut the pattern on paper first and then place it on the fabric.

When using a bordered bedspread as shown in the diagram, be sure to position the pattern correctly as the effectiveness of the border design depends on proper cutting. By cutting as shown, the border design forms a smart vertical pattern in back and down the back lap that wraps across the front.

The strips left after cutting both body pieces may be used for the ties instead of using ribbon or braid. You can either face the neck or finish it with a bias binding cut from the remaining fabric.

Another adaptation is to cut a higher neck and put a zipper in the back. You can also add either a soft bias roll collar or an oriental type stand-up collar if you wish.

Use velvet ribbon or one of the many interesting woven braids from Europe for the ties and neckline. If you choose a solid color fabric you can achieve handsome border effects by sewing ribbon or braid around the edge of the sleeves, down the front and around the bottom of the skirt.

METHOD OF CONSTRUCTION

Place the two back pieces together right sides in, aligning the border designs at the bottom, and sew the back seam. Then place the front and back pieces together, right sides in, align shoulder seams and stitch. Zigzag the raw edges of the seams if the cloth ravels easily. Otherwise they may be trimmed with pinking shears. Press the seams open.

Starting at the underarm cut, pin the curved edges together and sew from the sleeve edge to point A as indicated in figure 1. Pin and sew the side seams, then turn right side out. Pull the raw edges from A to B through the right side. Make a 1″ to

Figure 1

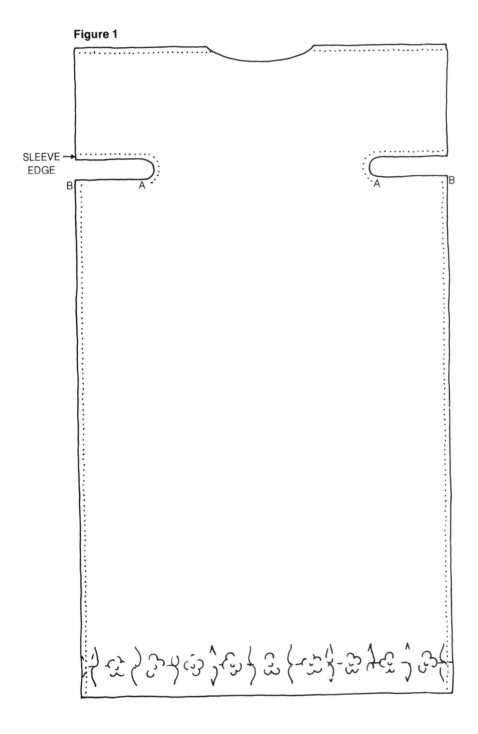

SLEEVE
EDGE

B   A

A   B

1½″ pleat including both the front and back of the lap using the border design as a guide for placing the pleat so that fold comes at the edge of the border. Use double woven cotton braid to sew over the raw edges, including the pleat of the underarm lap from A to B and extend the braid for long ties. Tiny bells at the ends of the ties add a nice touch (see figures 2 and 3).

Sew braid around the neck, leaving a free 3″ end at the left shoulder seam before starting to stitch and leaving another 3″ end when returning to the left shoulder. Tie the ends in a double knot and secure with needle and thread.

Hem the bottom of the garment and lastly top stitch the long edge of the front lap right through the hem at the bottom being careful not to stretch this seam.

If you wish to have the border design across the front edge of the sleeves as it is in the back, you can cut strips from the remaining cloth and sew them to the front edge of the sleeves, turning under the raw edges and top stitching into place.

Figure 2

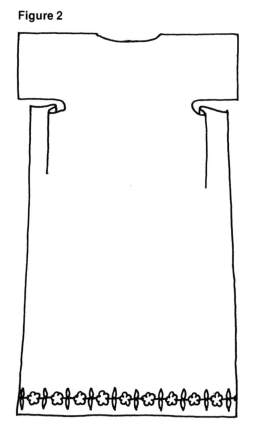

Figure 3

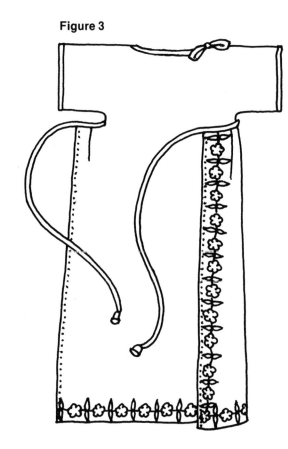

MONK'S ROBE

The process of accumulating patterns and designs is a delight and new ideas often come from the most unexpected sources. I discovered the monk's robe while reading a mystery story titled *The Tiger in the Smoke*. In it one of the characters found the following "recipe" written in old style English in the library of an old church:

> Of stout black woollen cloth take four equal pieces, each as long as the height of the Bro. from nape to heel, and as wide as will stretch across his shoulders from elbow to elbow. Let the first cover his left breast, the second his right, and the third shall cover him behind. Then let the fourth piece be folded into three, and of these, the first shall be for his left arm, the second for his right, and the third and last for his head. So shall he be covered and two ells of common rope encompass his middle.
>
> Reprinted from *The Tiger in the Smoke* by Margery Allingham, published 1973 by Manor Books, New York, N.Y.

I made several according to the exact specifications but found it is a better fitting garment if it is less wide, and now make a narrower version of it. To do this measure across the wearer's shoulders and down about 4″ or 5″ for a drop shoulder effect. Usually 25″ is wide enough for the average man; 20″ wide for women. Then cut four equal pieces to the desired length. One piece is the back, two pieces are the right and left front, and the fourth piece is cut first into three pieces for 2 sleeves and the hood. Since this makes the hood too deep, cut enough off the depth of the hood to make one or two pockets as shown in the cutting diagram.

FABRIC CHOICES

A soft blanket with a fleecy surface, or a bedspread, size 80″ x 108″ will make a warm, cozy winter robe. Lightweight East Indian bedspreads in solid colors or stripes are ideal for warmer weather robes or for beach wear. The nubby corded spreads in bright colors or stripes make especially good looking robes. Drapery materials are also suitable and can be very elegant.

FABRIC REQUIREMENTS

Bedspread 108″ x 80″ or
3 yards 45″ wide fabric or
2 yards 54″ wide fabric
Twisted cotton or silk rope cord for ties, if desired

CUTTING DIAGRAMS

BEDSPREAD OR BLANKET FABRIC LAYOUT

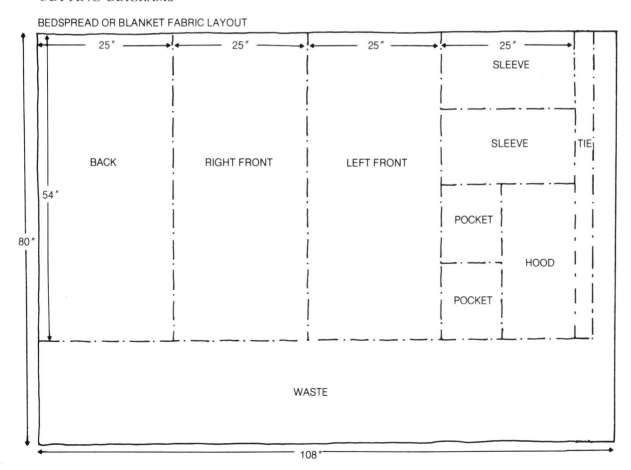

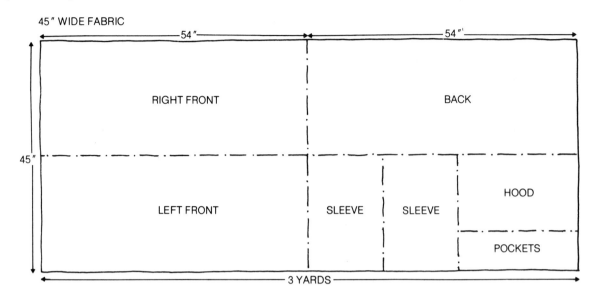

45″ WIDE FABRIC

54″

54″

RIGHT FRONT

BACK

45″

LEFT FRONT

SLEEVE

SLEEVE

HOOD

POCKETS

3 YARDS

If you are making this for a very tall person get 3⅓ yards and make each body piece 6″ longer than the diagram indicates. If you are using corduroy or velvet be sure to sew the body pieces with the nap all running in the same direction. Silk or cotton cord makes a nice tie belt with corduroy or velvet. Either a matching or contrasting color is effective. A cuff may be added to the sleeve for longer length if desired.

METHOD OF CONSTRUCTION

To finish both the inside and outside of the garment as you sew it together use a felled seam made as follows at the edges to be seamed. Press ¼″ under on the top side and press ¼″ up on the bottom side (figure 1). Place one overlapping the other ½″ and pin in position (figure 2). Stitch on one side, turn and stitch the other side creating a flat seam (figure 3).

Figure 1

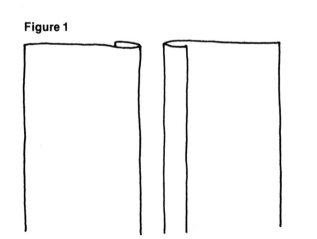

Figure 2

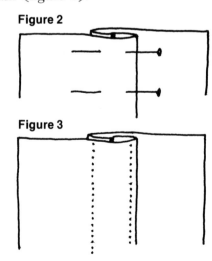

Figure 3

Mark with a pin the center (Y) at the top of the back piece. The first seams to sew are the shoulder seams. The sleeve edges of the shoulder seam are marked X in figure 4. Sew the right front and then the left front to the back from the edge X in to the middle of the back Y, leaving half of each front open where the hood is to be sewn.

of the hood at the center of the back (point Y) where the

Then fold the hood piece in half and make a seam along one edge to form the back of the hood (figure 5). Place the seam of the hood at the center of the back (point Y) where the shoulder seams meet and sew the hood to the top free edge of each side front (figure 6). If this seam is too thick to manage a flat felled seam you may bind it with matching double woven braid.

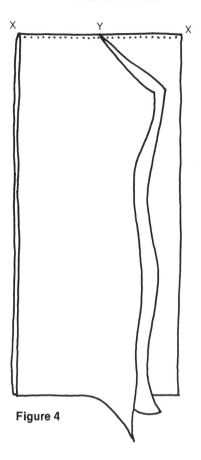

Figure 4

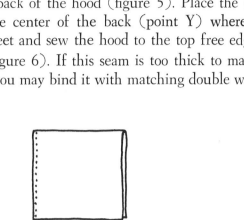

Figure 5

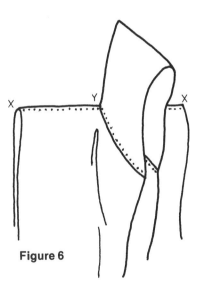

Figure 6

Fold each sleeve piece in half and mark the center point X with a pin (figure 7). Match the sleeve points X to shoulder seam points X and pin sleeves in place (figure 8). Join the sleeves to the body with flat felled seams.

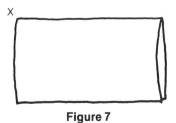

Figure 7

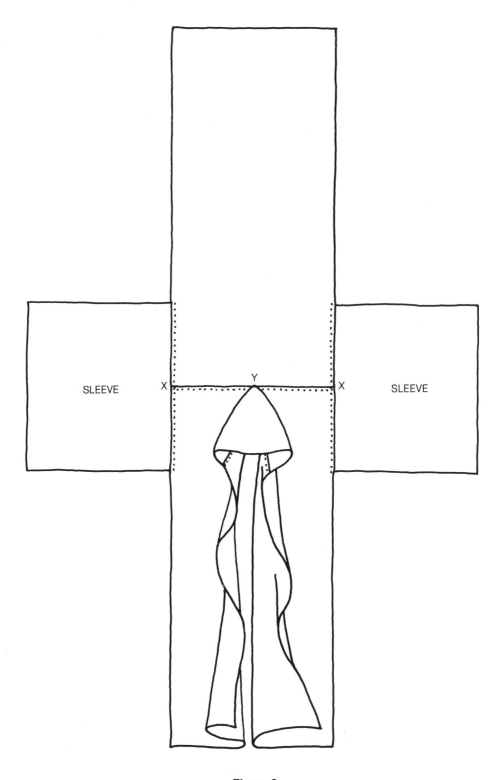

Figure 8

Then sew the underarm seams and the side seams all in one operation (figure 9). Hem the front openings, hood, and bottom of the garment all in one stitching operation. Hem the top edge of the pockets before attaching them. Place the pockets near the side seams at comfortable hand's reach and sew onto the robe, turning under the edges as you sew. Hem the sleeves.

If you want to make a tie belt of the same fabric hem all edges. You can add yarn fringe to the ends of the belt and a tassel to the tip of the hood.

Figure 9

MEXICAN TIE SKIRT

The Mexican tie skirt is a good example of how adaptable basic peasant designs are to contemporary fashions. The earliest version of this skirt was a straight tube of cloth which was pressed into pleats by hand and tied around the waist by a cord of cotton or leather (see figure 1a).

The first one I had was in the 1930s. It was mid-calf length, made of black cotton. One narrow tie held the front under-section in place and tied to the back. The back was gathered into a belt with tie ends that lapped across the front making a deep inverted pleat with a bow in the middle of the front (see figure 1b).

The directions and diagrams that follow are for a long version, ideal for evening wear at any time of the year.

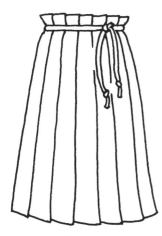

Figure 1a

Figure 1b

MATERIAL REQUIRED

2 yards 8″ of 36″ wide fabric, or
2 yards of 45″ or 54″ wide fabric

CUTTING DIAGRAM

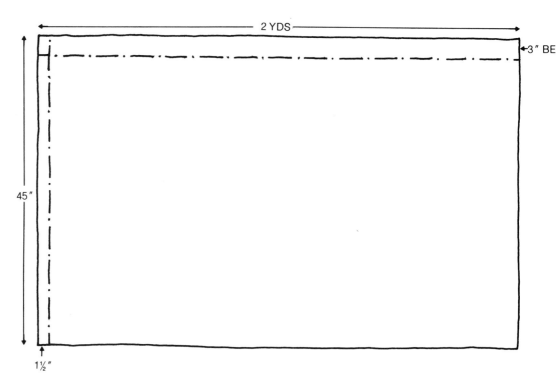

For this design I prefer a 45″ wide border print cotton. The border around the bottom of the skirt adds greatly to its beauty. Handwoven striped fabric is also handsome and can be found in import shops selling fabrics from Mexico, Guatemala, Peru, etc. The vertical stripes make a lovely skirt. A soft wool plaid is great for a colder climate.

METHOD OF CONSTRUCTION

Fold the skirt in half, right side in, with the border print across the bottom, and pin the edges together carefully aligning the border print. Sew a ½″ seam from top to bottom.

Turn the skirt right side out. Step into the circle of the skirt. Pull the top up to your waistline, placing the seam at the right side 3″ from where a right side seam would ordinarily be. Measure across the front to within 3″ of where a left side seam would be and mark this point B with a pin (see figure 2).

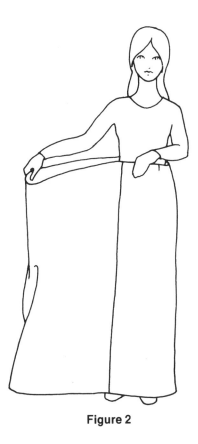

Figure 2

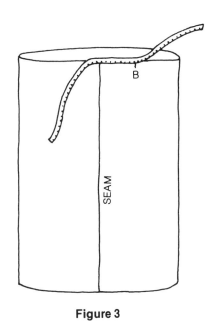

Figure 3

Now take the 1½″ x 42″ tie piece and mark the center of it. Place the center point of the tie right side down against the right side of the center front of the skirt and sew the tie in place from the seam to point B. Turn the tie over, fold in the raw edges, and top stitch along the entire length to finish the tie ends (figure 3).

Now step into the skirt again, center the front, and tie the front section in place. From point B start measuring across the back circle of the skirt to place four darts, one at each side and two in the middle of the back (figure 4). Three inches to the left of point B pin a dart (figure 5) where the left seam would be. Proceed 5″ or 6″ and pin in another dart. Proceed 5″ or 6″ and pin in the third dart, then another 5″ or 6″ further pin in the dart where the right side seam would be. This allows a little extra fabric so the skirt can be slightly gathered between the darts to the tie belt. The darts, of course, should be inverted and sewn on the wrong side. Make each 7″ long.

Figure 4

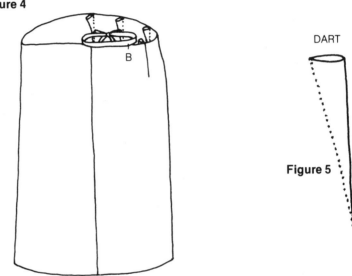

DART

Figure 5

After the darts are sewn, step into the skirt again and tie it in place. Then pull the remaining loose fabric at the top of the skirt straight out to the right side and mark that point A (figure 6). You will have a loop which will pull across to the left side B to form a lapped skirt. The front section of the loop from A to the seam should be equal to the distance from the seam to B. Make a ¼″ hem along the top edge of the loop from A to the seam (the underneath section of the lap that will cross over the front).

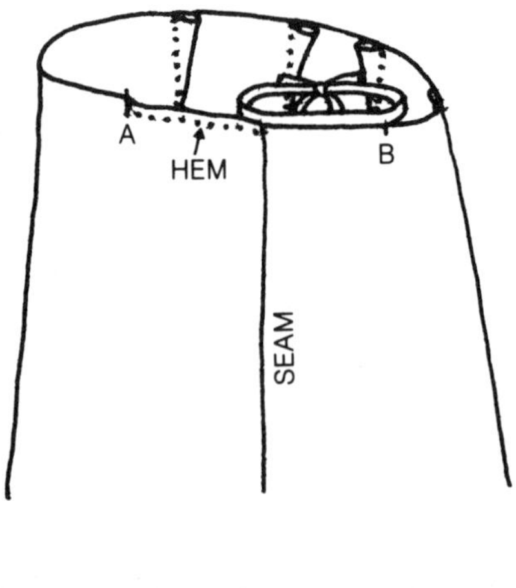

Figure 6

A

HEM

B

SEAM

Figure 7

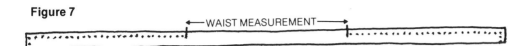

—WAIST MEASUREMENT—

Before continuing with the skirt, prepare the belt (figure 7). First fold the strip of fabric in half lengthwise, right side in; place the center of the strip against the center back of your waistline, bring the ends of the strip around to the front center of your waistline and mark those points with pins. Sew across one end of the strip and along the edge to the point marked with a pin. Do the same on the opposite end, leaving the center section unsewn. Turn the strip right side out and press. The belt from A to B must be your exact waist measurement.

Then using the largest, loosest stitch on your machine, or making running stitches by hand, sew around the top edge of the back of the skirt from B to A (figure 8). Pull the thread gently to gather in the extra fullness all around and pin this gathered edge to one open edge of the belt, and baste in place. Bring the other open edge of the belt to the inside skirt edge, turn under the raw edge and baste in place. Secure the belt by top stitching from end to end (figure 9).

Step into the skirt, tie the narrow under belt around to the back, lap the right side from A to B on the left, and tie the outer belt (figure 10). Measure the length and hem the bottom of skirt.

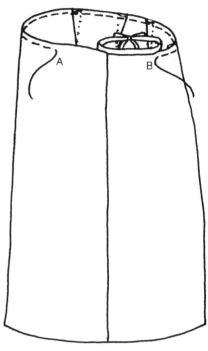

Figure 8

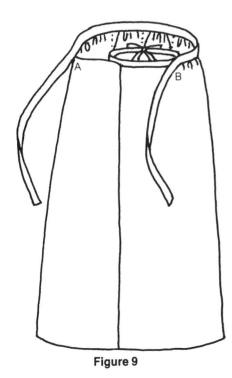

Figure 9

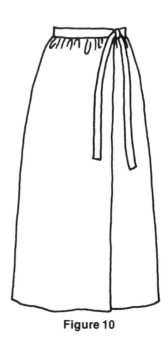

Figure 10

AFRICAN KUTU

The kutu, based on a traditional African design, is one of my favorite garments because it is so simple to make and so glamorous to wear. It should be made of reversible fabric since the cape portion reveals both the top and underside. But if you should fall in love with a design printed only on one side, don't rule it out because you can always line the cape portion from the shoulder fold to the bottom edge. Be sure to choose a fabric that falls gracefully and drapes well—any soft cotton, silk, wool, jersey, or synthetic fabric.

The kutu can be worn as is in warm weather, or over a long-sleeved turtleneck shirt or body suit in cooler weather.

MATERIAL REQUIRED

2⅓ yards of 45" wide fabric (for street length dress; 3 yards for long dress)
20" piece of ¾" wide elastic

CUTTING DIAGRAM

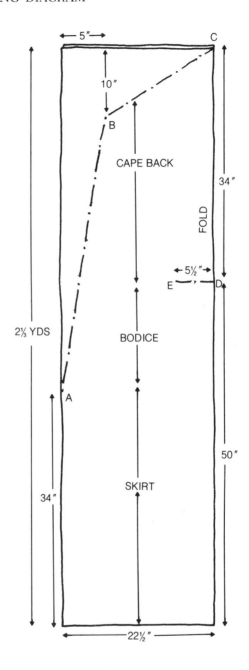

Before cutting, fold the fabric in half lengthwise, right side in.

The lengths specified in the cutting diagram are approximate. Point A indicates the back of the waistline. Point D, which is 16″ above the waistline, indicates the shoulder line and neckline. Before cutting the neckline slash from point D to point E, measure the distance from your waistline to your shoulder line, and mark the fabric accordingly.

As you can see from the diagram, a single piece of fabric forms the skirt, bodice, and cape back. The kutu can be made from a simple rectangle with the cape back squared off across the bottom. This adaptation calls for a slightly tapered cape that comes to a graceful point at the back. The cape also may be made as long as the garment itself—an adaptation that is particularly becoming to an ample figure.

METHOD OF CONSTRUCTION

After cutting the fabric, before unfolding it, machine sew a seam from the waistline (point A) down approximately 26″ as shown in figure 1. This seam will fall at the center back of the dress (see figure 2). The unsewn portion serves as a slit to make walking easier.

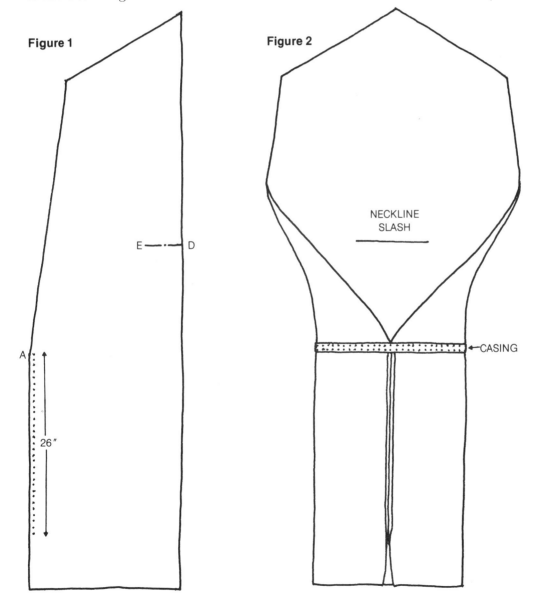

Figure 1

E ——·—— D

A

26″

Figure 2

NECKLINE
SLASH

←CASING

From the leftover fabric cut a straight piece 28″ long and 1½″ wide, which will be used as a casing for the elastic to gather in the sides and back. Also cut several 1″ wide bias strips and sew them together to make one strip approximately 25″ long, which will be used to face the neckline.

Slip the neckline slash over your head to make sure it is wide enough to get in and out of comfortably. If you prefer a rounded neckline, cut away the fabric to the desired depth in front and back. Measure the length around and add to the bias strip if necessary.

To face the neckline, pin the bias strip right side down around the right side of the neck opening, and machine sew ¼″ in from the edge. Turn the bias strip in to the wrong side, turn under the raw edge, and sew to the body of the garment using whip stitches.

Now turn the garment inside out, center the casing strip at the center back seam, turning under the raw edges, and baste it in place (see figure 2).

Turn the garment right side out and top stitch the casing in place. Turn inside out again and sew one end of the elastic firmly to one end of the casing. Then run the elastic through the casing, gathering in the fabric as you do so. Pin the end of the elastic to the other end of the casing and try on the kutu before sewing the elastic in place.

To put on the garment fold the cape down in front and step into it through the opening at the waistline. Pull up the garment until the waistline is in place and then slide the neckline opening over your head. The cape will fall into place in back and form sleeves of a sort on either side (see figures 3a and 3b).

While you have the kutu on adjust the elastic at the waistline, letting it out or pulling it in more to suit your measurements. The back and sides should be pulled in enough to hug the body without pulling the fabric tight across the front. The 15″ wide section not pulled in by the elastic should fall smoothly. At the same time measure the hem and pin it in place.

Sew the other end of the elastic firmly in place, hem the bottom of the skirt, and make a narrow hem around the entire cape section (see figure 4).

Worn with a handsome pendant or African barter beads, the kutu is ethnic elegance at its most dramatic.

Figure 3

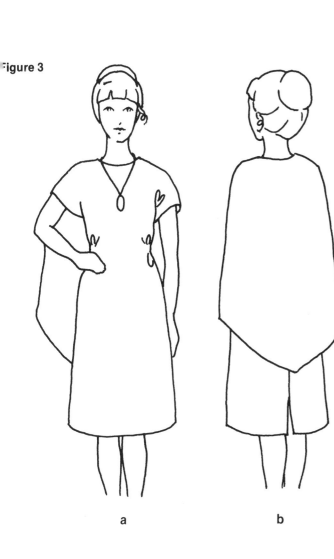

a   b

Figure 4

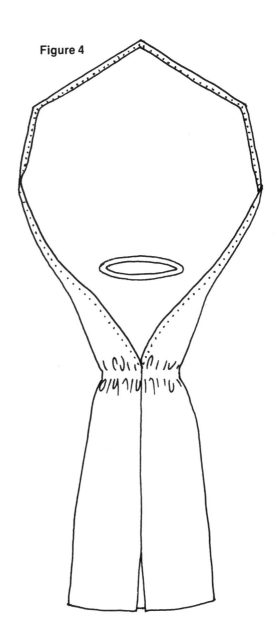

EARLY AMERICAN PATCHWORK SKIRT

Patchwork is an old and appealing craft that transforms scraps of used, and otherwise unusable, material into richly patterned fabric. It was particularly popular among the early settlers in America and some of the quilts that have survived from colonial days now hang as works of art in museums.

The most intricate, beautiful patchwork designs are simple to make since all that is involved is seaming together the various individual pieces of material. Of course, if you happen to have an old patchwork quilt that you don't mind cutting into, it would make a lovely skirt. I have made patchwork of cotton, wool, and velvet, sometimes combining all three in one large piece. One very elegant skirt combined burgundy, rose, and dark green velvet with satin of the same color—the overall effect suggested medieval stained glass.

Dip into your scrap bag for a variety of colors and prints, or if you prefer a planned color combination buy two-thirds of a yard each of three coordinated fabrics.

The instructions that follow are for an easy-to make, attractive skirt that wraps to the back and ties in front. This is a slimming design with a long straight line.

MATERIAL REQUIRED

⅔ yard each of three different 45″ wide fabrics
1⅝ yards of lining material (cotton, rayon, or synthetic)
3½ yards of 1½″ wide grosgrain ribbon

Cut or tear the fabric into 7″ squares. For a medium size skirt (10 to 14) you will need fifty-four 7″ squares, nine strips of six 7″ squares each.

CONSTRUCTION DIAGRAM

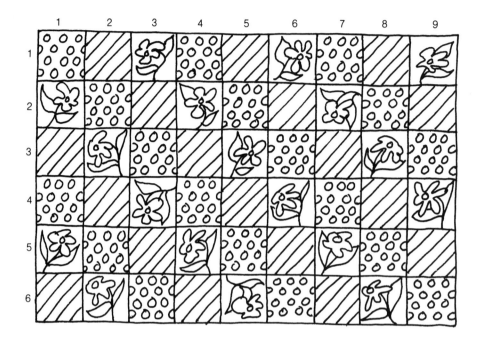

If you want the skirt to be longer and larger around, use seventy 7½″ squares, ten strips of seven squares each. For smaller sizes (5 to 9) use fifty-four 6½″ squares.

METHOD OF CONSTRUCTION

Place all the pieces right side up on the floor, bed, or large table top and plan the design of each strip. Machine sew the squares together into strips. Spread out the strips, decide in what order you want to join them to achieve the design you wish, and then number each strip so there is no chance of becoming confused when you begin to sew them together. Start at the top and join each new strip to the one above it.

When the patchwork piece is complete, cut the lining the same size as the patchwork. The lining may be pieced at one end if necessary. Placing the lining and patchwork together, right sides in, machine sew the bottom of the lining to the bottom of the patchwork piece (figure 1).

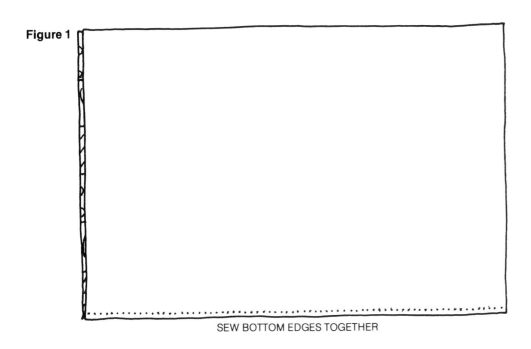

SEW BOTTOM EDGES TOGETHER

Then measure the skirt against you and turn under the patchwork piece to the desired length. This will bring the top edge of the lining an inch or two above the top edge of the patchwork (figure 2). Cut off this excess strip. Leaving the fabric wrong side out, align the seams at either end and sew by machine (figure 3).

TURN UP HEM WIDTH & TRIM TOP

Figure 3

ALIGN EDGES & SEW SIDE SEAMS

Turn the fabric right side out, align the top edges, and pin in place. Then make a row of running stitches along the entire top edge of the skirt and lining (figure 4).

Figure 4

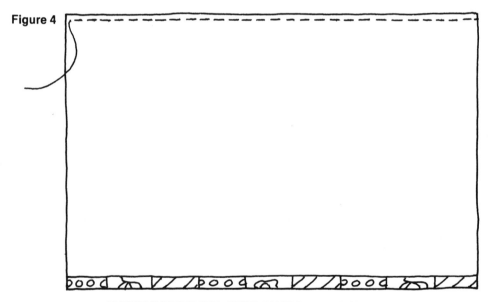

TURN RIGHT SIDE OUT, PRESS, MAKE RUNNING STITCHES AT TOP

Cut a 36" piece of ribbon, and mark the center of this piece. Mark the center of the remaining piece of ribbon. Place one piece of ribbon on top top of the other, matching the center points, and top stitch along the upper edge (figure 5).

Pull the running stitches to gather the skirt to a 36" width, slide the gathered edge into the opening between the two pieces of ribbon, pin in place, and top stitch the ribbon waistband to the skirt (figure 6). This leaves 27" of ribbon at either end to wrap and tie.

Figure 5

CENTER

Figure 6

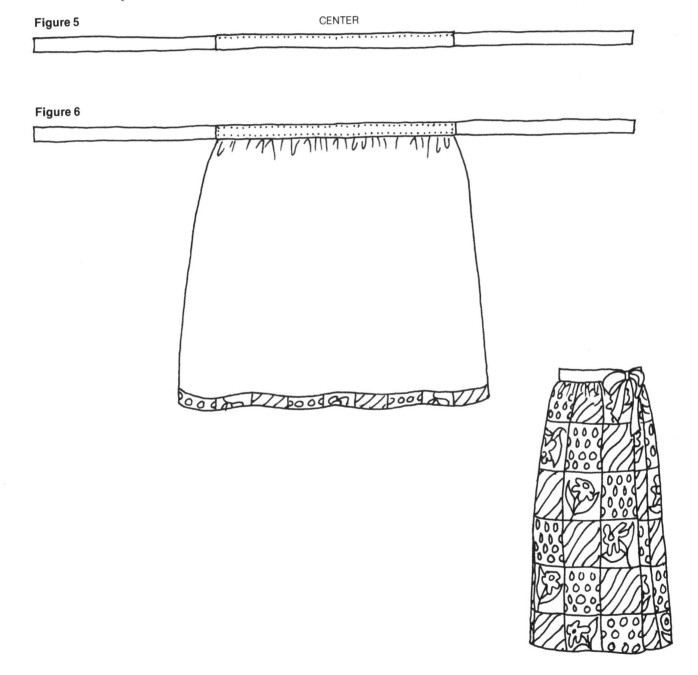

BASIC KAFTAN

One of the most classic and versatile shapes in ethnic garments is the kaftan. The basic design that follows is of oriental and middle eastern origin. It is characteristic of the traditional garments worn by the Chinese, Persians, Arabians, and East Indians.

The garment may be made short or long, large or small, of heavy or sheer material, and the ways of enhancing its beauty with decoration are endless. The measurements suggested are for medium size and will fit sizes 12 to 14 (bust measurements to size 36 and hips 33″ to 40″). The finished garment should hang gently from the shoulders and move easily on the body with room to spare. It should measure at least 10″ to 12″ larger around than your own largest measurement. You may make the neckline large enough to slip over the head or you may have a short opening in front to close with buttons and loops or buttonholes. Or you may make an opening down the entire length of the front and sew in a zipper leaving a slit at the bottom. If you want it to look as authentic as possible decorate the opening with braid and embroidery. Along one side of the opening sew dozens of tiny round brass buttons. Along the opposite side sew an extra row of braid with loops already woven into it to fasten the buttons. This type of braid can be purchased readymade.

The Chinese version often has a side and shoulder opening and a mandarin collar. Handmade frogs or tiny brass buttons and loops are the fastenings. You can simulate this effect by decorating one shoulder and side with braid and close the garment with a seam and zipper down the back.

I have decorated several kaftans with top facings of beautiful print fabrics in bright colors and others with appliqué

(DOUBLED)   SINGLE   (DOUBLED)

8"   16"   6½"

20" SLEEVE

X

BODY
BACK

20" SLEEVE   X

FOLD

4"

4"

CUT 4" SQUARE
GUSSETS IN HALF
DIAGONALLY

FACING
(CUT DOUBLE
ON FOLD)

SHOULDER
LINE

FOLD

3½ YDS.   X

CUT
ALONG
FOLD
AND
NECK
CURVE

BODY
FRONT

5"   5"

CUTTING DIAGRAM

54"   54"

SIDE PANELS
(CUT ALONG
CENTER LINE)

13"   13"

designs cut from an old paisley shawl, using embroidery stitches
to unify the decorative details and the body of the garment.

In addition to using decorative braid at the openings it is
interesting to define all seam lines with braid or yarn. I often
use a contrasting 4-ply yarn and just run it ahead of the needle
as I machine stitch it to the garment.

Depending on the fabric and trimming used, the basic kaftan
can serve as a casual hostess robe or an elegant evening wrap.

MATERIAL REQUIRED

3½ yards of 45" wide fabric
embroidery thread and/or braid to trim neck opening and
seams (optional)

METHOD OF CONSTRUCTION

Place the body of the garment flat with the right side up. Pin the facing in position, right side down, along the front opening and neckline and machine sew in place (figure 1).

Clip the raw edges at the curves and points so the facing will not pull when it is turned. Then turn the facing to the wrong side of the garment and press.

Hem the raw edge of the facing and then anchor it to the garment with loose whip stitches. You may find it convenient to sew on whatever decorative trim you plan to use at this point since the garment is less bulky now than when fully constructed. If you decide to do so, see page 114 before continuing.

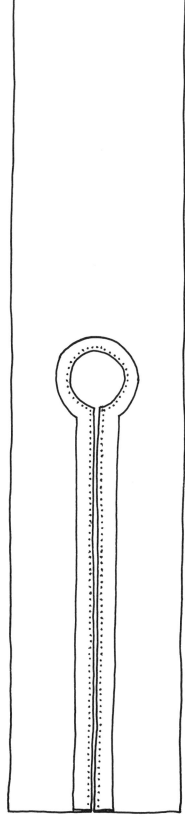

Figure 1

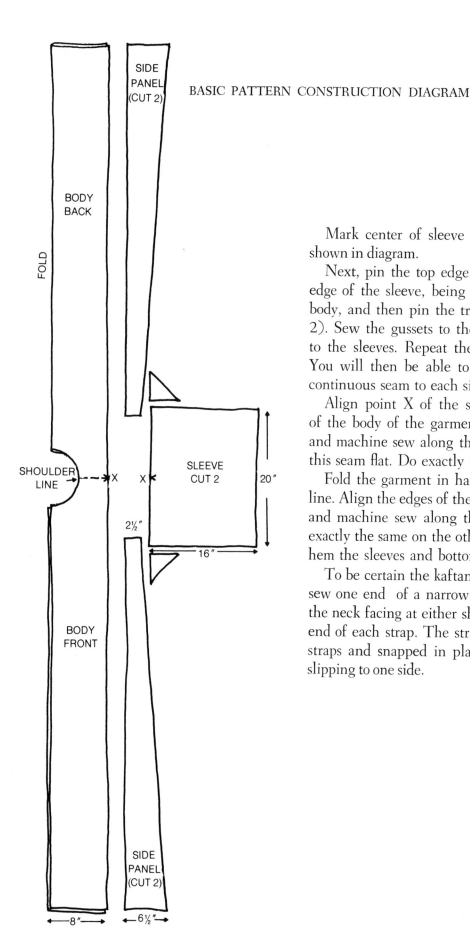

Mark center of sleeve edge and shoulder line points X as shown in diagram.

Next, pin the top edge of each side panel to the underarm edge of the sleeve, being sure the straight edge is toward the body, and then pin the triangular gussets in place (see figure 2). Sew the gussets to the panels and the panels and gussets to the sleeves. Repeat the same operation on the other side. You will then be able to sew the sleeves and panels in one continuous seam to each side of the body of the garment.

Align point X of the sleeve with point X (shoulder line) of the body of the garment, right sides together, pin in place and machine sew along the entire length (see figure 3). Press this seam flat. Do exactly the same on the other side.

Fold the garment in half, right sides in, along the shoulder line. Align the edges of the panels, gussets, and underarm seam, and machine sew along the entire length (see figure 4). Do exactly the same on the other side. Press all seams flat and then hem the sleeves and bottom edge.

To be certain the kaftan stays in place across your shoulders, sew one end of a narrow, inch-long strap to the underside of the neck facing at either shoulder line. Sew a snap to the other end of each strap. The straps can then be slid under your bra straps and snapped in place to keep this wide garment from slipping to one side.

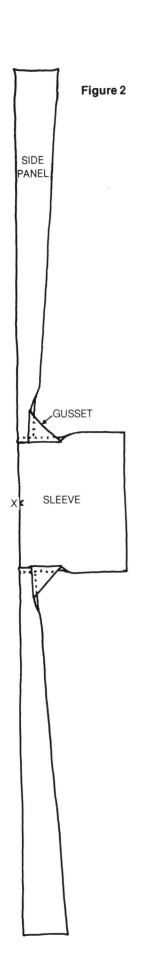

Figure 2

SIDE
PANEL

GUSSET

X

SLEEVE

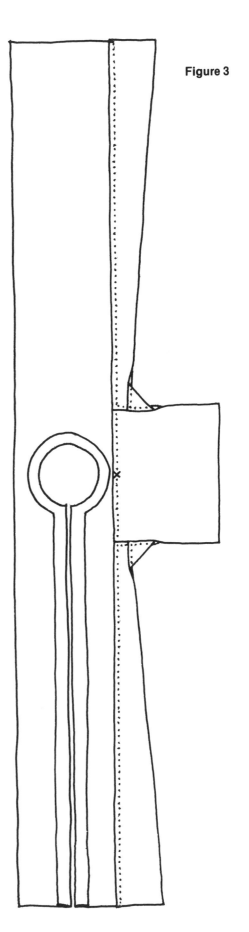

Figure 3

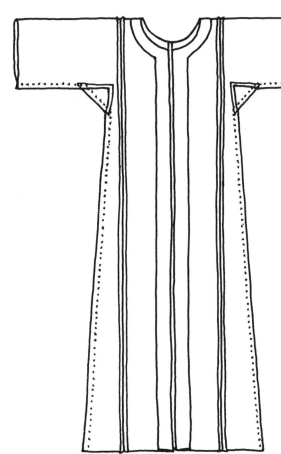

ADDING DECORATIVE DETAILS

I made a particularly handsome kaftan of soft, light-weight navy blue wool appliquéd with paisley designs cut from an antique shawl which was too worn in places to be usable. The designs were appliquéd down the length of the opening, flaring out along the shoulder fold and continuing down the back to make a deep V shape. After finishing the appliqué work I embroidered around each design in yarn to match the kaftan, using outline and free-fly stitches. Then, using yarn to match one of the soft red shades of the paisley designs, I delineated all seams as described on p. 8.

Several rows of woven braid sewn along the length of the opening, around the neck, and around the edges of the sleeves add an attractive decorative touch. I have, on occasion, cut a top facing of an interesting fabric and sewn it to the body of the garment with braid edging.

You may want to embroider down the whole length of the kaftan using a combination of modern and old sampler type embroidery stitches. The garment becomes a magnificent heirloom when embroidered by your own hands using your own design ideas.

Handwoven fabric with an elaborate design worked right into the middle of the width makes a lovely kaftan. The design will run down the front and the middle of the back.

LINING

If you wish to line this garment choose a soft cotton or synthetic fabric and cut and sew it together as you did the kaftan. Pin the finished lining into the kaftan and sew it in place with whip stitches along the front opening, around the neck, and at edges of the sleeves. Hem the bottom of the lining an inch shorter than the kaftan and anchor it with French tacks at the bottom of each seam.

KAFTAN VARIATIONS

Many variations of the basic kaftan can be made simply by using the full width of the fabric, altering the neckline and side seams as suggested in the following diagrams. They may be short or long. The short versions make lovely tops for pants or skirts, and, depending on the fabric, can even be used as aprons, cover-ups, or smocks.

Variations 1, 2, 3, and 4 are *very* simple. You can make a more formal garment by adding cuffs—either narrow ones as shown in figures 5 and 5a, or wide ones that gather the fabric in to form the equivalent of sleeves (see figure 5b).

When tapering the bottom of the kaftan for a narrow effect, as in variation #4, leave a slit at one or both sides for walking ease.

MATERIAL REQUIRED

   3½ yards of 45″ wide fabric
   braid, tassels, embroidery yarn (optional)

CUTTING/SEWING DIAGRAMS

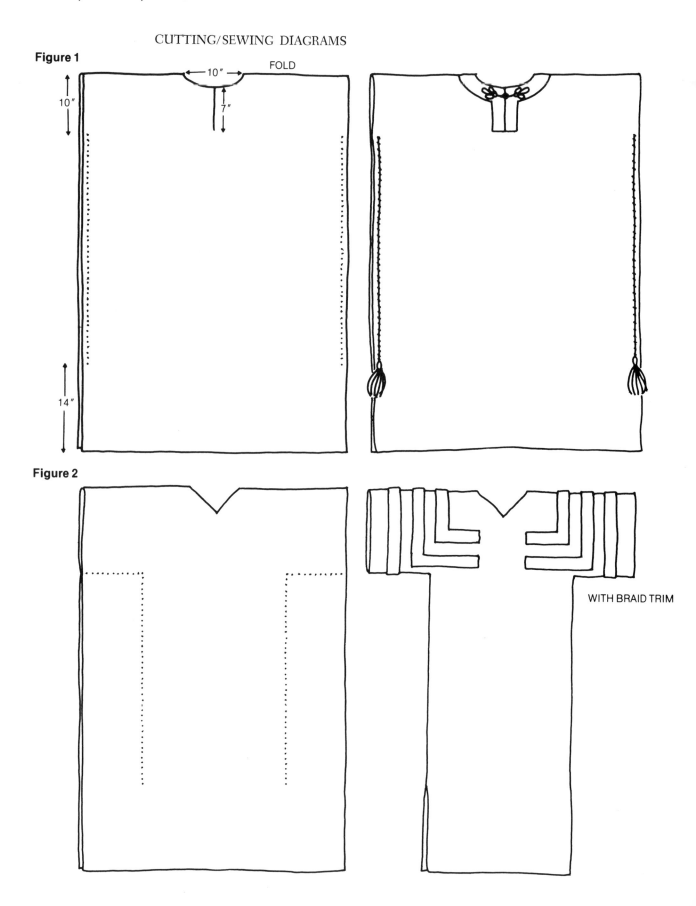

Figure 1

FOLD

10″

10″

7″

14″

Figure 2

WITH BRAID TRIM

Figure 3

FOLD

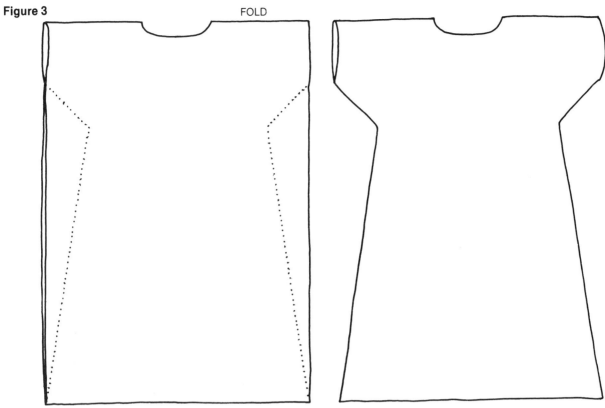

Figure 4

LEAVE
BOTTOM
14″
UNSEWN
FOR
SLITS

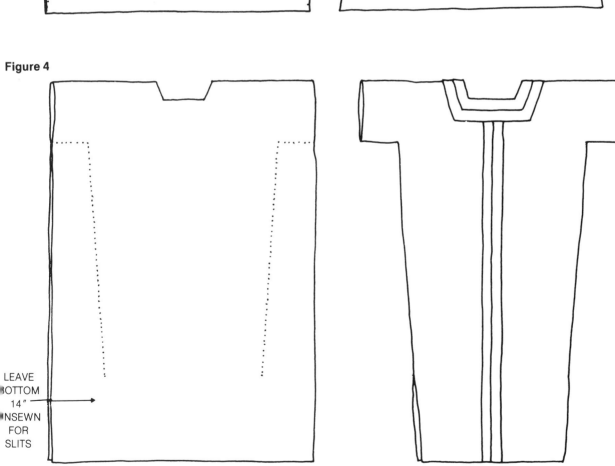

117

Figure 5

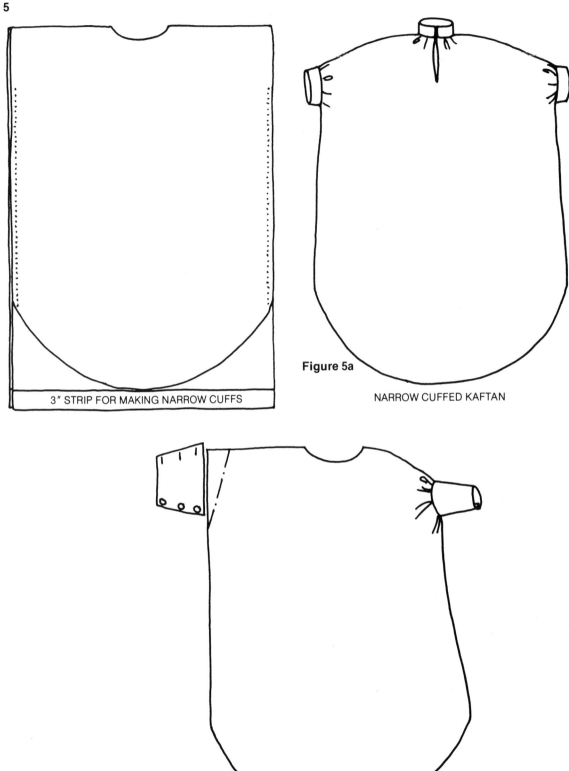

3" STRIP FOR MAKING NARROW CUFFS

Figure 5a

NARROW CUFFED KAFTAN

Figure 5b

FABRIC GATHERED INTO CUFFS TO FORM SLEEVES

Kaftan variation #6 is lovely made of silk or challis print, or plain wool or cotton trimmed with an Indian mirror embroidery yoke. These elaborately embroidered, mirrored yokes are available in many import stores. I found a yoke with mirrors and black and yellow embroidery which I used on a kaftan of yellow bonded wool, and the effect was striking.

MATERIAL REQUIRED

3½ yards of 45″ wide fabric
24″ neck opening zipper

CUTTING DIAGRAM

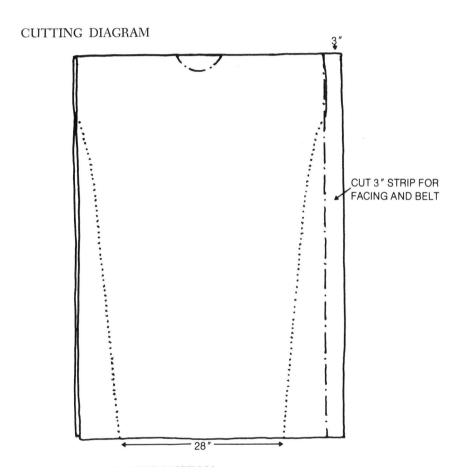

3″

CUT 3″ STRIP FOR
FACING AND BELT

28″

METHOD OF CONSTRUCTION

First cut a 3″ strip the full length of the fabric. Then use the remaining 42″ width for the kaftan.

Taper the side seams from the bottom of the armholes to a 28″ width across the bottom. Slit the back the full length and then machine sew a seam leaving 24″ open at the top for a zipper and 12″ to 14″ at the bottom for a slit. Use part of the 3″ strip to face the slit (see figure 6a).

Hem or face the neck and sleeve edges, and hem the bottom.

Now measure down in front from the center of the neckline to your waistline. From that point X (see figure 6b) measure 5″ to either side and make a 1¾″ vertical slit. Finish the raw edges of these slits with buttonhole stitches.

To make the belt, fold the remaining 3″ strip of fabric in half lengthwise, right side in. Machine sew across one end and along the entire length. Then turn the strip right side out, turn in the unsewn end and sew closed by hand.

Slip the ends of the belt into the slits so that the front of the garment is gathered in at the waist, and tie the belt in back underneath the kaftan (see figure 6c).

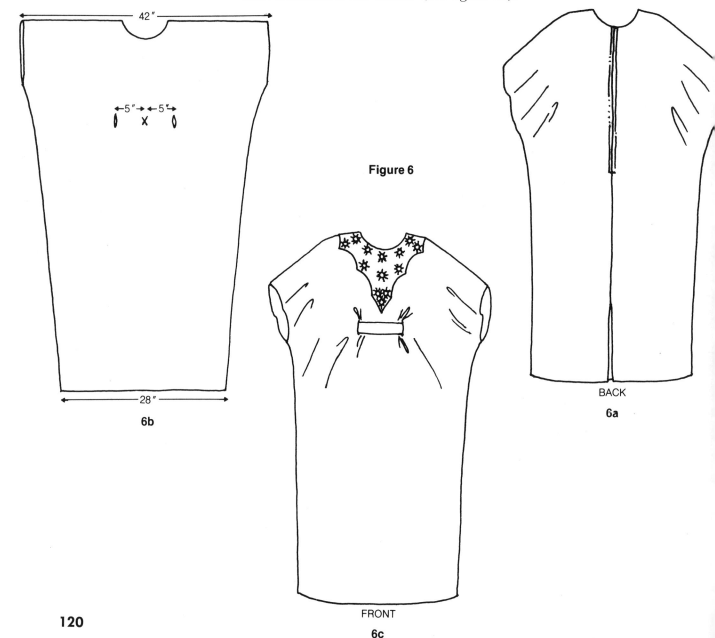

Figure 6

6b

BACK

6a

FRONT

6c

DANISH
CAPE DRESS/TOP

This cape dress is based on an ancient design. I adapted it from the drawing of a shirt (see figure 1) dating back before the first century found in an archeological dig in Denmark. The shirt probably was made from animal hide and was worn by putting the head through the neckhole, wrapping the short front lap around to the back and tucking the bottom edge into a skirt held on by thongs tied around the waist.

In the basic pattern shown below I have made the cape part and the front longer to be worn as a dress, but have also made a shorter version cut several inches below the waist in front to wear with pants (see figures 2a and 2b). The front is buttoned in back under the cape, which is longer than the front. The sleeve front is sewn down against the cape in back with the stitches running from the outside edge to approximately under the armpit on each side. This leaves the arms surprisingly free while the cape moves gracefully with your body as you move.

MATERIAL REQUIRED

2¾ yards of 45″ wide fabric
½ yard of ¾″ wide elastic
3¼ yards of fringe, braid, or other trim (optional)

CUTTING DIAGRAM

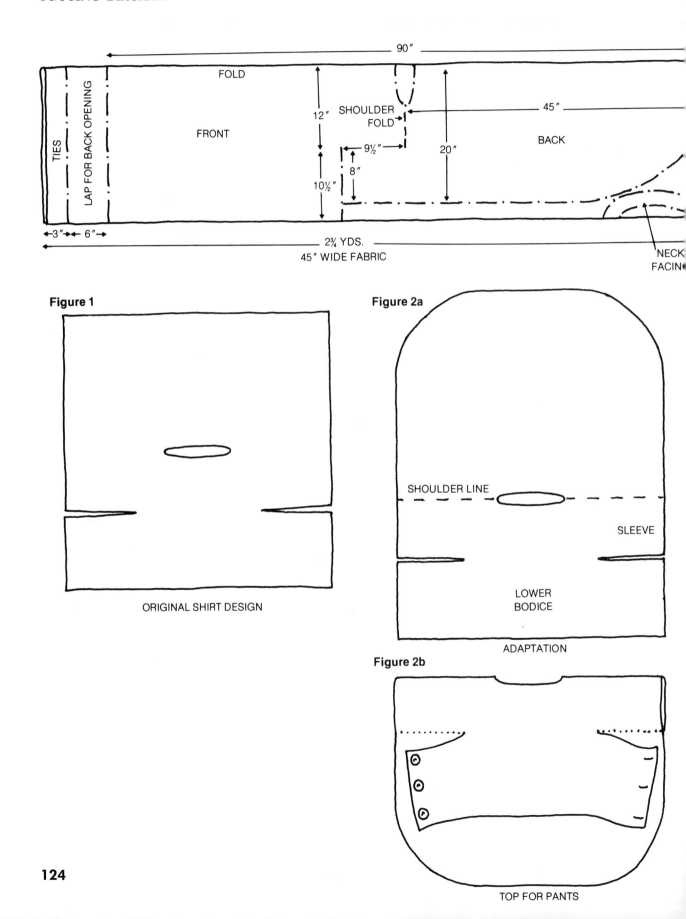

Figure 1

ORIGINAL SHIRT DESIGN

Figure 2a

SHOULDER LINE

SLEEVE

LOWER
BODICE

ADAPTATION

Figure 2b

TOP FOR PANTS

METHOD OF CONSTRUCTION

First face the neckline as it will be easier to handle the bulk of the fabric before the garment is stitched together. Then make a ½″ hem around the sleeve/cape piece from point A to point B (see figure 3).

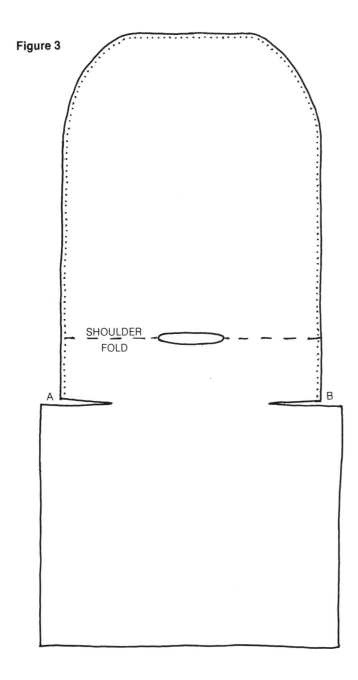

Figure 3

SHOULDER
FOLD

A

B

Next find the shoulder line fold, then pin and stitch the underarms of the sleeves to the cape in back, turning under the raw edges before sewing. Sew from the outer edge in for 8″ on either side to form the sleeves (see figure 4).

Make a ½″ hem along the side edges of both front flaps and across the bottom of the front (again see figure 4).

Then make a 1″ hem across the top edges of both flaps, using the regular seaming stitch on your machine since these hems will serve as casings for elastic and therefore should be very firmly sewn (again see figure 4).

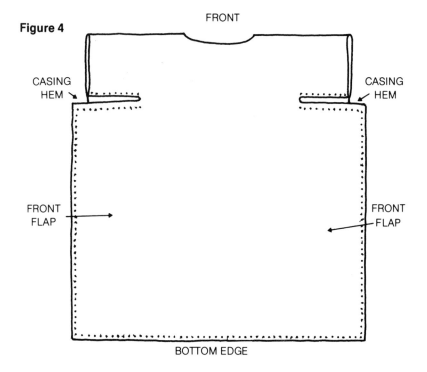

Figure 4

FRONT

CASING HEM

CASING HEM

FRONT FLAP

FRONT FLAP

BOTTOM EDGE

Cut two 7″ long pieces of elastic. Run the elastic through the casing on each side, and stitch firmly in place at the underarm and outer edges. This will gather in the fullness of both flaps, as shown in figure 5.

Next take the 45″ x 3″ strip and cut it in half to make two 22½″ x 3″ strips, which will serve as ties. Fold each strip in half lengthwise, right side in, sew across one end and along the length; turn right side out and sew the open end. Sew the ties firmly to points C and D of the front flaps as shown in figure 5.

Take the 6″ strip you cut earlier and cut it to a length of 34½″. Make a ½″ hem at the top and bottom and along one side. Join the unhemmed edge of this piece to the left front flap as shown in figure 5. This will serve as an extra lap of

Figure 5

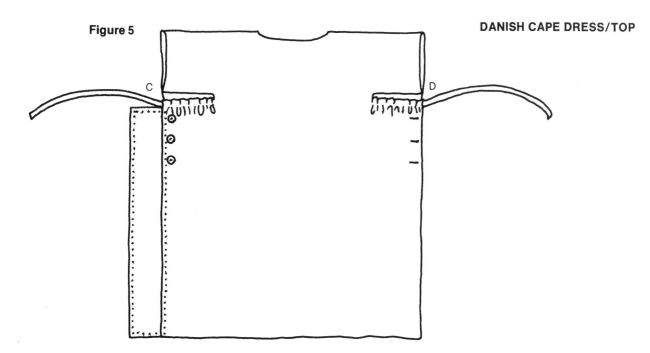

fabric at the back opening of the skirt. Make three buttonholes along the edge of the right front flap, and sew on three buttons along the left front flap as shown in figure 5. The ties hold the skirt in place in back, but the buttons are needed to keep it securely closed (see figure 6).

Figure 6

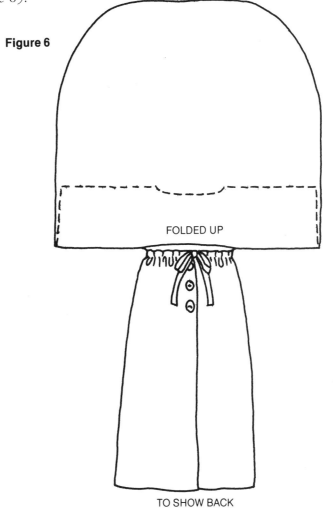

FOLDED UP

TO SHOW BACK
UNDER CAPE

At this point you are ready to add whatever decorative details you choose—fringe, braid, applique, embroidery, etc. I recommend sewing fringe around the sleeves and along the edge of the cape, and embroidering a scroll design at the neckline, as shown in figures 7 and 8.

This cape dress can easily be made ankle or floor length by extending the length of the front and the cape. And the cape can be made shorter or longer than the skirt. This would make an unusual, interesting wedding dress made of handwoven cotton, heavy silk, or lace, with a long trailing cape.

Figure 7

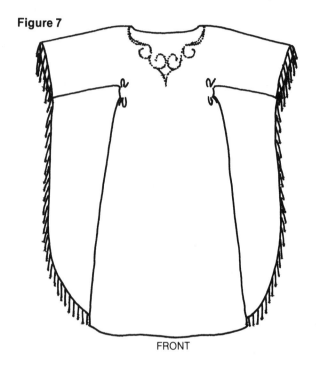

FRONT

Figure 8

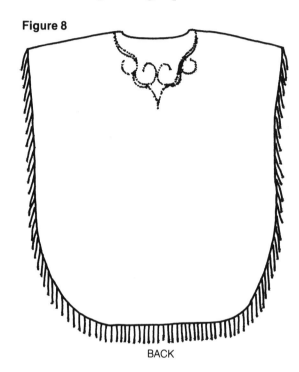

BACK

VENEZUELAN
DRESS AND OVERSKIRT

The traditional dress and skirt worn by Venezuelan Indian women have always intrigued me. The wrap-around and tie overskirt is a practical garment that must have evolved to protect the more fragile, lighter colored dress underneath. The typical dress is white, and the skirt black, worn with bright shawls and sashes to liven the effect. Lace at the neck and sleeves, probably a Spanish influence, adds soft decorative touches to the otherwise simple lines of the dress.

The following adaptation can be made in a wide variety of colors and fabrics. I chose a white crinkly cotton for the dress and trimmed it with coarse white cotton lace. From the leftover fabric I made a long tie, trimmed with lace at either end to use as a sash when wearing the dress without the overskirt. The overskirt was made of the same crinkly cotton in a deep blue shade. The side opening of the skirt shows the dress underneath as you walk, and makes the garment comfortable to move in. This version of the skirt and dress is slightly less full than the traditional Venezuelan costume—again, for comfort and convenience. An embroidered border around the bottom and up the sides of the skirt adds a colorful accent.

This is a wonderful outfit to take with you on a resort holiday as it can be worn several ways or combined with other things. The wrap skirt is a handy cover-up to wear over a swim suit or around your shoulders as protection from the sun or chilly breezes. The dress alone, or with the overskirt, is perfect for late afternoon and evening wear. In a pinch, you can even use the dress as a nightgown.

MATERIAL REQUIRED

3½ yards of 36″ wide fabric (for dress)*
2½ yards of 45″ wide fabric (for skirt)*
3 yards of 3″ to 4″ wide lace
1½ yards of ½″ wide elastic
embroidery thread or 5 yards of decorative braid (optional)

CUTTING DIAGRAM—DRESS

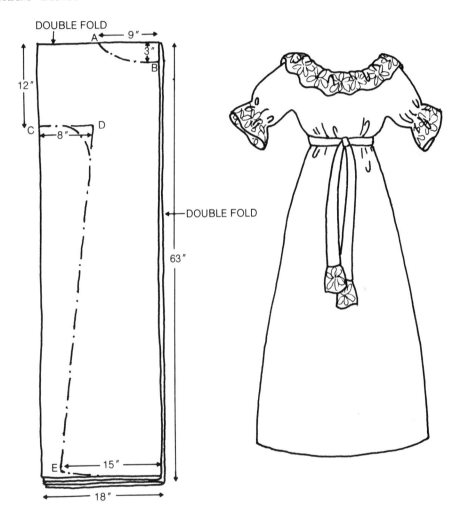

*(Use preshrunk fabric. Fabric requirements are based on average height—5′ 3″ to 5′ 6″. To determine fabric needs for anyone shorter or taller, measure twice the length from shoulder to floor, plus 4″, for the dress; and twice the length from waist to floor, plus 4″, for the skirt.)

FOLDING AND MARKING DIRECTIONS

Fold the fabric in half vertically, and then in half again horizontally. Measure and mark points A, B, C, D, and E as indicated in the cutting diagram. Note that point E is 1″ up from the bottom edge, and that the cutting line under the arm from point C to point D should be gently curved. Cut all four layers of fabric at the same time.

From the leftover fabric cut several lengths of bias strips 1½″ wide, and a long straight piece to use as a sash.

METHOD OF CONSTRUCTION

Stitch the underarm and side seam on each side in a single operation. Reinforce the underarm with a second row of stitches and clip the edges of the curved section to ease any tension in the fabric (see figure 1).

Next pin and sew the bias cut strips together (see figure 2) to make one long facing strip approximately 36″ long, and press the strip flat. Turn the dress right side out, place the facing strip right side down around the neckline, and machine sew

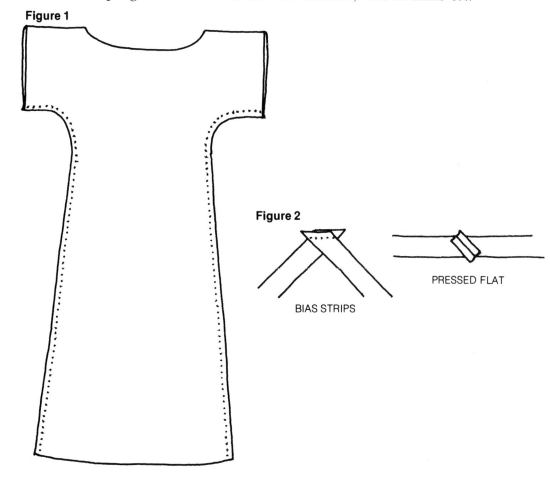

Figure 1

Figure 2

BIAS STRIPS

PRESSED FLAT

in place ¼″ in from the edge. Turn the strip over to the inside of the dress, turn under the raw edge, and machine sew in place ¾″ in from the neckline edge. Leave approximately 1″ of the facing unsewn since the facing will serve as a casing for the elastic, which will be run through the unsewn opening.

Cut a piece of lace long enough to go around the neckline, plus 2″. Join the end of the lace with a felled seam so no raw edges show. With the dress right side out place the lace right side up against the top edge of the neckline and machine sew it in place all around. Then run a length of elastic through the casing, gathering in the neckline to a comfortable width and depth. Sew the ends of the elastic together firmly by hand and close the small opening in the casing with several whip stitches.

Next make a ¾″ hem around the edge of each sleeve, leaving approximately 1″ unsewn since the hem will serve as a casing for the elastic, which will be run through the unsewn opening. Treat the sleeve edges exactly as you did the neckline, sewing on the lace and running elastic through the casings.

Hem the bottom edges of the dress to the desired length.

Piece together the sash with felled seams, make a narrow hem all around, and add a piece of lace at each end. This can be tied at the waist or just under the bosom when wearing the dress alone.

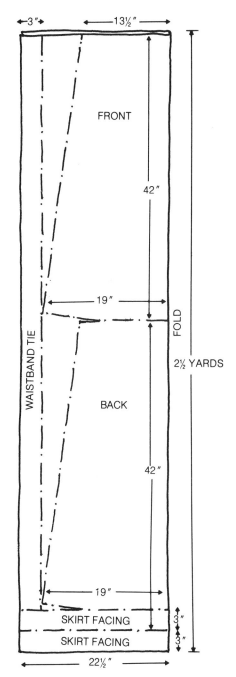

CUTTING DIAGRAM–SKIRT

METHOD OF CONSTRUCTION

Open out the front and back pieces and join them together with a seam along one side (see figure 3).

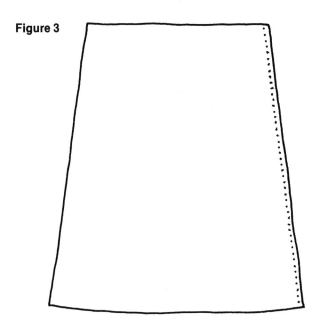

Figure 3

Trim the skirt facings to the same length as the skirt. Place the facings, right side down, against the right sides of both skirt edges and machine sew in place (see figure 4).

Turn the facings to the wrong side of the skirt, press the sewn edges flat, turn under the raw edges, and sew the facings against the body of the skirt with whip stitches.

Figure 4

Next, make a row of running stitches along the entire top edge of the skirt, gathering in the fullness to fit your waistline (see figure 5). Then take the waistband tie, fold it in half lengthwise, turn under the raw edges ¼", and press the whole thing flat. Position the gathered edge of the skirt in the center of the tie, pin or baste it in place, and then top stitch along the entire length of the tie and across both ends.

Measure the skirt to the desired length—either the same length as the dress, or shorter if you want the bottom of the dress to show below the skirt—and hem by hand.

Now the skirt is ready to be trimmed with whatever decorative details you wish to add—machine or hand embroidery, readymade woven braid, rickrack, hand crocheted braid, fringe, or a combination of several.

You may also want to consider lining the skirt with a bright print or contrasting color to make it reversible.

Figure 5

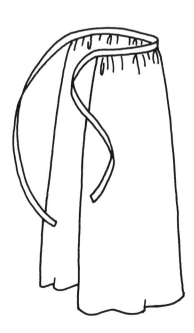

HEIRLOOM MOSAIC SKIRT

First select the most beautiful scraps you can find among your leftover fabrics from other sewing projects or from favorite old garments ready to be discarded. They can be widely varied as long as all the pieces are compatible in color and texture.

You may use cotton, wool, velvet, satin, or almost any non-stretchy material. I prefer using fabric with similar textures in a skirt, although satins or silks and velvets go well together. If using velvets for this particular skirt it is not necessary to keep the nap all going the same direction. The light catches the texture from different angles and gives the skirt a delightful shimmer as you move about.

Using a piece of good acrylic lining fabric, cut out your favorite skirt pattern and seam it together with the raw edges facing out. The rough seams will be covered by the pieces

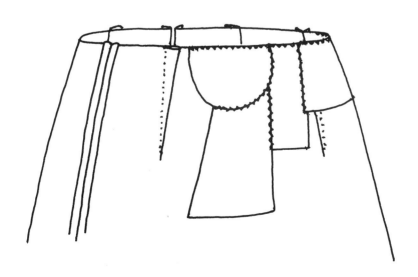

stitched on top. Starting at the top, sew each piece to the lining using the zigzag stitch on your sewing machine. Place one piece down just under the bottom edge of the piece above it so the zigzag stitches will sew both pieces together at one time. Use pieces of varying sizes and shapes—some large, some small—trying to place complementary colors together. You need not turn the edges under as these will be covered later by either embroidery or braid.

When you have covered the lining with a rich mosaic of fabrics, the skirt has a quilted look because of all the stitching. Now add the waistband, hem the bottom, and cover the machine stitching with braid or embroidery stitches.

This skirt is well worth the time it takes to make—it is eye-catching and perennially chic.

MEASUREMENT CHART
METRIC EQUIVALENTS TABLE

MEASUREMENT CHART

Shoulder width	
Bust	
Hips	
Thighs	
Neck	
Around upper arm	
Around wrist	
Length from shoulder to hemline (short)	
Length from shoulder to hemline (long)	
Length from waist to hemline (short)	
Length from waist to hemline (long)	
Length from underarm to wrist	
Length from shoulder line to tip of bust	

METRIC EQUIVALENTS TABLE

METRIC TO ENGLISH

1 centimeter = .4 inch
1 meter = 3.3 feet
1 meter = 1.1 yards
1 square meter = 1.2 square yards

ENGLISH TO METRIC

1 inch = 2.5 centimers
1 foot = .3 meter
1 yard = .9 meter
1 square yard = .8 square meter

Index